Interior Decorating 101

Home Decorating & Staging Course

Volume II

Illustrations, Photos, & Text
by Shirley Lise

Published by
Lise Publishing
1 Elgin Court, St. Marys, ON
N4X 1A1

Copyright© 2013, All rights reserved

ISBN: 1494332051

Interior Decorating 101

Home Decorating & Staging Course

Volume II

The second of two units of study preparing a student for a career in Interior Decorating and Home Staging as well as equipping those who value good decorating in their own home.

about the Author

I am an avid Canadian gardener, landscaper, and home decorator, having studied and obtained a diploma in both Interior and Landscape Design, as well as having gained valuable experience via hands-on projects in both fields. Just recently, I have put my pen to the test to develop curriculum for courses in both these areas of expertise, and have produced a self-help instructional garden manual, *Easy Front Yard Gardening*, as well as *Interior Design Basics* and this complete Interior Decorating course presented in a series of two units of study, **Interior Decorating 101** Volume I and **Interior Decorating 101** Volume II previously published as *Interior Design For Today*.

Adding to my writing portfolio, I have also begun blogging in order to reach an audience of followers and to potentially stir their enthusiasm for home décor and garden design. **Home Décor Blog Book** Volume I is a compilation of home décor blogs up to date.

In all my endeavours, my intent is to share what I have learned with others, to equip them, and to encourage them to develop a passion for decorating and landscaping. My hope is that you will enjoy this hands-on Interior Decorating course, while at the same time, gain the skill and knowledge needed to qualify as a home decorator.

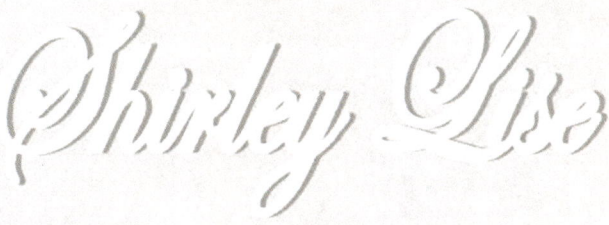

Contents

08	DESIGNING AROUND ARCHITECTURAL FEATURES
21	DESIGNING WITH COLOR
46	DESIGNING WITH FABRIC
61	COMPLETING A COLOR SCHEME
83	DESIGNING WITH WINDOW TREATMENTS
95	DESIGNING WITH WALL TREATMENTS
102	DESIGNING WITH FLOORING
120	KITCHENS AND BATHROOMS
160	THE INTERIOR DESIGN PROJECT
166	RE-DESIGN AND STAGING
180	THE INTERIOR DESIGN PRESENTATION
206	YOUR OWN INTERIOR DESIGN BUSINESS

Designing around architectural Features

When considering a space, not all rooms are created equal! Some rooms have overbearing features that restrict the designer in style, architectural detail that dictates, lines that challenge furniture placement in the room. In this lesson you will learn how to design your furniture layout around these room details. You will learn how to **Camouflage** unwanted *"negative"* detail and how to **Accentuate** *"positive"* features in the room. You will be reminded that harmony in style and mood are required in any design scheme, and that designing around architectural features of a room incorporates these principles. Elements we will be considering are the **Shape of the Room** and **Architectural Detailing**. Special attention will be given to **Tricks of the Trade** in **Altering Perception** of a room.

On entering a room, train your eye to observe features in the room. Look at the shape of the room and note any variations, alcoves, juts in the wall, bulkheads, posts, window bays, or any other unusual shape of the space. You will need to decide if these features are "positive" or "negative," and if they need to be **Camouflaged** or **Accentuated**.

What if the room has angled corners? Would you consider this to be a "positive" feature in the room, and decide to accentuate it? You can draw the eye to it with the placement of four matching sconces mounted in the center of each corner.

What if the room is an "open concept" design that opens into other areas of the home? How will you design around this feature? Unless you are planning to close the room in to treat it as a separate space, you will treat this feature as positive and work with it. To bring harmony into the space, you will want to incorporate design features, such as furniture style and color palette, from adjoining rooms into your design scheme.

What if the ceiling is a soaring Cathedral ceiling? You will gladly take advantage of the light and airy feeling. You will consider this as a most positive feature and will design a scheme that "fits" with this architectural feature of the room, leaning toward a modern, contemporary style.

Look at the windows in the room. Is there a big "Picture" window or a "Bay" window. These are architectural features of very positive nature. You will want to accentuate them, framing them with draperies that enhance their beauty and draw attention their way. The "Bay" window can be further enhanced by building a seating area below it known as a "Window Seat." Refer to the BAY WINDOW TREATMENT for help.

The room shape features we have just discussed are positive features, however there are features that will be decidedly negative and you will want to de-accentuate them.

BAY WINDOW TREATMENT

What if there is a support column in the middle of your room. You cannot remove it. You may not consider it a positive feature, and will likely decide to camouflage it. This is where the **Tricks of the Trade** come in. To hide, or camouflage a feature, in needs to be blended into its surroundings. To accentuate a feature, it needs to stand out by contrasting it to its surroundings.

One way to camouflage a support column is to paint it the same color as the walls to blend it in. Another way to camouflage it is to build a wall, partition, or room divider around it, thus hiding it as well as overcoming its negative quality of being a safety hazard.

Another "negative" feature in a room would be a wall column that distracts and makes the room feel unbalanced. Camouflaging it with built-in cabinets on either side will cause the column to disappear. If the column is on a window wall, it can camouflaged by incorporating it into the window treatment, hiding it behind a full wall treatment of draperies. Still another way to disguise a single unbalanced colum, is to add a symetrically placed second column in the room to off-set it and bring balance.

Another negative feature would be a jut in the wall. In order to overcome the negative quality of imbalance to the wall, you might decide to accentuate it with a built-in cabinet, closet, or if the width of the recessed wall portion is significant, you might want to develop it as your focal point in the room. Refer to your DESIGNING AROUND ARCHITECTURAL FEATURES help for more detail of how to use this architectural detail to your advantage.

What if the room has "bulkheads," lowered portions of ceiling, housing heating ducts or electrical wiring? These, on first look, might be considered negative features to be camouflaged, however, with some creative flare, these can become very positive features in the room. For instance, if there is enough "headspace," or room in the bulkhead to install recessed downlights, you can bring a much appreciated form of lighting into your room as a functional or mood enhancing element.

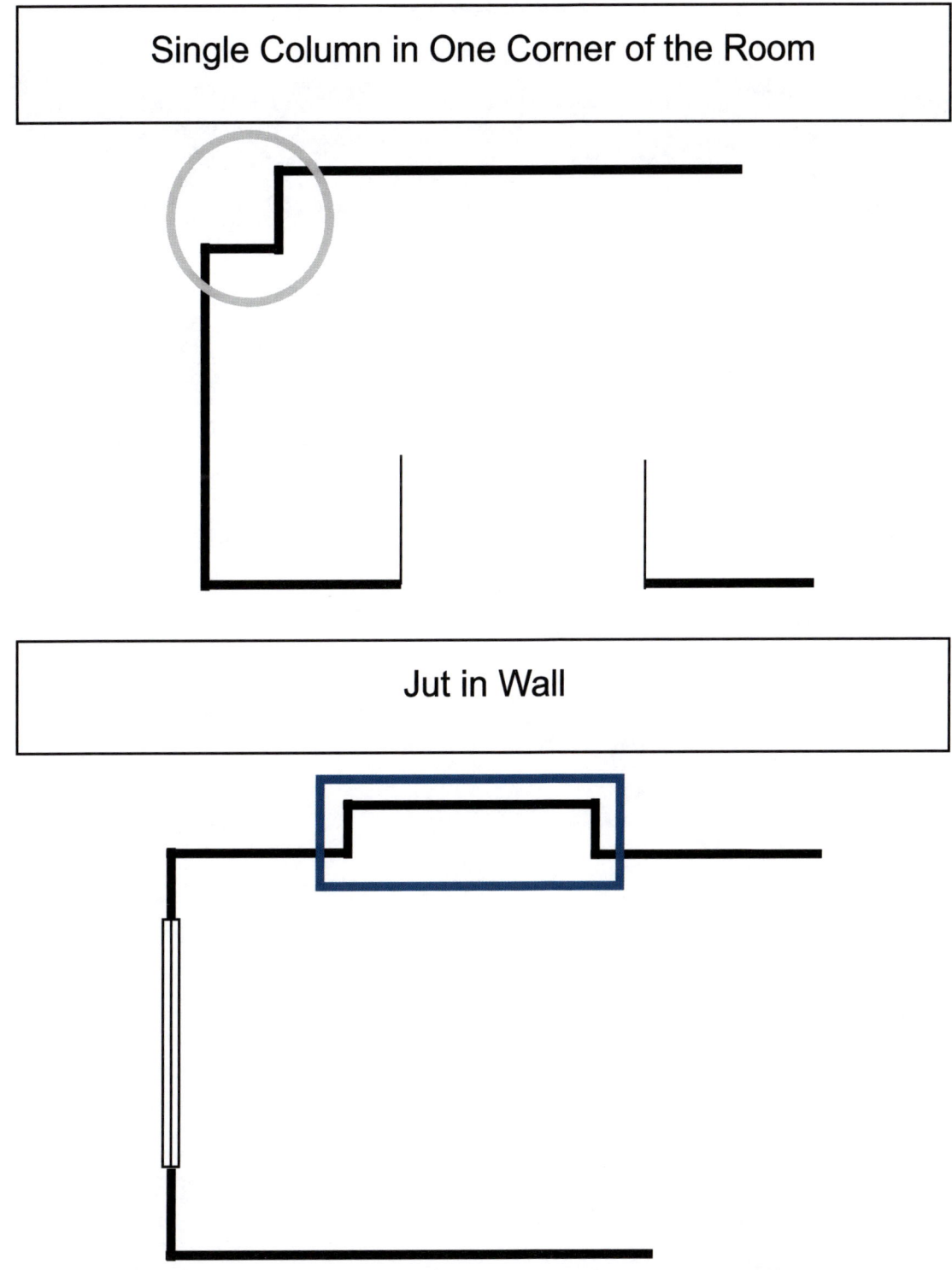

DESIGNING AROUND ARCHITECTURAL FEATURES

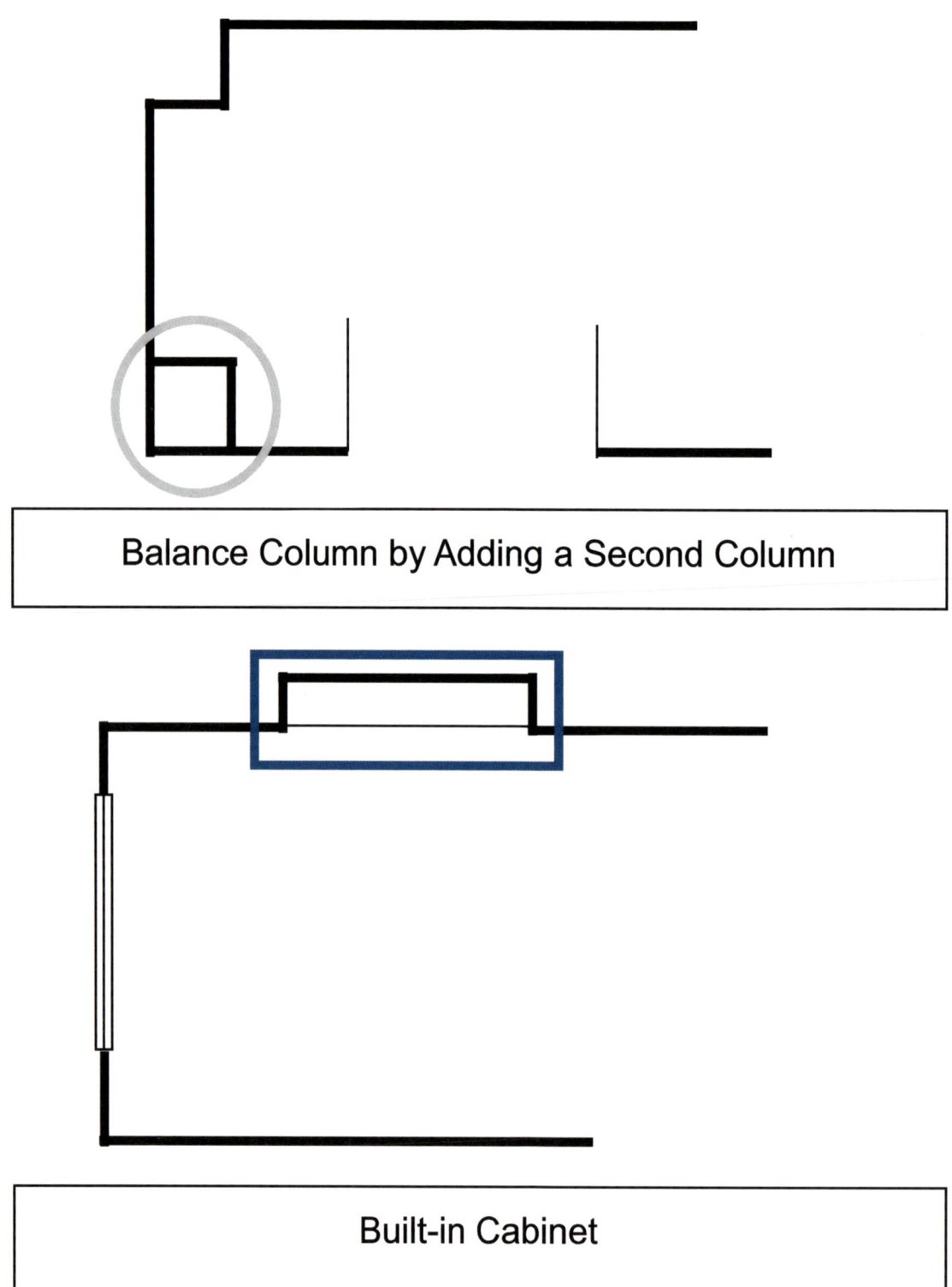

Balance Column by Adding a Second Column

Built-in Cabinet

DESIGNING AROUND ARCHITECTURAL FEATURES

Architectural Detailing

A second architectural element you will need to consider when you are planning your interior design, is the **Architectural Detailing** of the room. You will need to decide if the detail will enhance your design, or hinder it. You will also need to decide if you will remove it, or work with it, accentuate it, or camouflage it.

Does the room have distinctive detailing in style? Does the room exude a certain style through the architectural details in it? Does the room have an English, French or Early American flavor to it. If so, elements in the "decorative" detail of the architecture will define it. English and French style ceilings, for example, may be decorated with heavy beams or engraved tin. A dining room might have an ornate center moulding and Crown moulding. These elements, unless removed, will dictate the style of the room.

Another feature of detail that dictates style to a room is its Trimwork. Are the trim, mouldings, baseboards, and doors in a room elaborate or of no consequence?

In order to design around such architectural details in a room, principles of camouflage apply. That is, to hide, or camouflage a feature, in needs to be blended into its surroundings. To accentuate a feature, it needs to stand out by contrasting it to its surroundings.

If you want to create a modern, contemporary style in the room, you will want to remove or camouflage ceiling and trimwork detail by painting it out in the same color as the ceiling or walls to blend it in. If you want to keep the dictates of these details and incorporate them into your design, paint them a contrasting color.

Tricks of the trade can be applied to problem solving when it comes to various aspects of a room. You have already been familiarized with one trick of the trade, the principle of blending in by *"camouflaging"* and making a feature stand out by *"accentuating"* it. A second trick of the trade is to alter a feature's *"Visual Perception."* This trick can be used in addressing ceiling height.

Altering Visual Perception of a Room

1. "Lowering" a High Ceiling

When you walk into a room, you must determine if the ceiling height is in harmony with the size of the room. If it is too high, you will want to alter its visual perception. You will want to make it appear lower. In order to do this, you must apply the principle of "Line." Vertical lines create height, while horizontal lines take away from height. In interior design you can apply this principle to visually lower your ceiling height.

One way to do this is to add horizontal mouldings such as Crown or Picture moulding. Paint the trim and mouldings in a color contrasting to the walls to emphasize them. The eye will be drawn across the room instead of up the room.

When using wallpaper, you may choose to use a horizontal pattern, or break it up with a Chair Rail, applying the paper below the railing and painting the wall above.

Another way to "visually lower" a ceiling is to paint a border around the top of the room in the same color as the ceiling. Because dark colors make things appear closer, do not use white on the ceiling, but use a muted color from your room color scheme.

To visually enhance the room with a lowered feature in the ceiling, consider building a "bulkhead," a framed and drywalled portion of ceiling

added to the original ceiling. This is a good choice in kitchen design, where recessed lighting is installed to illuminate a selected portion of counter, usually over the sink or bar area.

Another way to draw the eye down and away from a high ceiling without adjusting the architectural features, and especially effective during night time hours, is to use hanging fixtures and downlighting.

2. "Raising" a Low Ceiling

What if the ceiling is too low. If the room is small, a lower ceiling will not be a problem, however, if the room is spacious, a low ceiling will not be in proportion to its size. The ceiling height of the room will then be considered too low and tricks of the trade will be needed to make it appear higher.

You will want to de-emphasize horizontal lines in the room. If the room has Chair Rail or Wainscoting, either remove it or camouflage it by painting it the same color as the wall.

Bright colors tend to recede, so paint the ceiling white. And if using wallpaper, carry it from floor to ceiling. Striped patterns are best as they emphasize vertical lines.

3. "Altering" Room Proportion

Is the room small, or is it large? Is it too small, or too large? Is it long and narrow? There are several ways to change the visual proportions of a room.

Follow rules regarding color. Dark colors appear to advance, while light colors appear to recede. Using dark color on the end walls and light color on the long walls of a narrow room will make the room appear wider.

Using dark wall colors will make a room appear smaller, while light wall colors will make the room appear larger, therefore, to make a small room appear larger, use light color on the walls. To further visually expand the space, keep coherence in the room. Unify the color scheme by painting all the walls and trim the same color and use window treatments that blend in with the walls rather than stand out against them. Solid colored draperies are better than prints, however, if a print is chosen, the print should be small with the background color matching the wall. Blinds should also appear subtle with narrow slats and in a color matching the wall. Continue the unified look in the room by using the same window treatments on all the windows in the room.

Use of small scale furniture with light solid-colored or small-patterned fabrics will also give the sense of more space. Seamless wall-to-wall carpeting is preferred over area rugs which break up the space. Keeping the room uncluttered with a minimal amount of furnishings and using mirrors and other reflective surfaces in the decorating scheme will also visually expand a small room.

If the room is too large, the opposite approach to the small room can be taken to make the room appear smaller. Large-pattern, rather than small, darker colored walls instead of light, and diversifying elements of the decor as opposed to unifying the room, will bring success.

Break up continuity with mouldings in contrasting co-ordinated color, or paint one of the walls in a second co-ordinating color, or wallpaper it. Using different treatments on the walls will break coherence and make the room appear smaller.

Window treatments in a large room need to fit the scale of the room, therefore, big and bold drapery patterns are appropriate. Although keeping draperies and painting trims in a co-ordinating contrasting color to the walls will visually break up the space, the same window treatments should be used on all the windows.

Use large-patterned area rugs rather than wall-to-wall carpeting. Fill the space appropriately to scale with large-scale, large-patterned, or highly-textured upholstered furniture and enough pieces so the room does not look empty. Take care however, not to use both a bold-patterned rug with bold-patterned upholstery that competes with it, but either one or the other.

AfterRoom Perception

Designing with Color

*I*n this lesson, you will learn about **Primary, Secondary,** and **Tertiary Hues** and the **Color Wheel**. You will study the **Value** and **Intensity** of color, and how color is applied to produce mood. Special consideration of lighting and color undertones will be addressed. You will learn how to put together a color scheme and design using each of a **Monochromatic**, **Adjacent**, **Complimentary**, **Triadic**, and **Tetradic Color Palette**.

Primary Color

Hue is the pure color of a pigment. The word hue can be used interchangeably with the word color.

There are three **Primary Hues**, red, yellow, and blue, from which all other colors are produced. When you mix red and yellow, you produce orange. When you mix blue and yellow, you produce green. When you mix red and blue, you produce violet (purple). These six colors are **Secondary Hues**, and when put into a circle, form a **Color Wheel.**

Complimentary Color

Refer to the following COLOR WHEEL for help. Notice that red and green are opposite on the color wheel. If you combine red, yellow, and blue, you will produce a neutral brown. Green is composed of blue and yellow, therefore, if you mix green and red, you are actually mixing together all three primary colors and they will produce brown. Because red and green "complete" each other, that is, they turn brown when mixed, they are considered **Complementary Colors**.

Observe that violet is opposite yellow on the color wheel. They too can be mixed together to produce brown, and therefore are also complementary colors, just as blue and orange.

Tertiary & Intermediate Hues

All hues produced halfway between a primary and a secondary color are considered **Tertiary Hues**. They can be mixed to varying degrees. For instance, if red and yellow are mixed, they produce orange. If a greater amount of red is used than yellow, the combination becomes a color between red and orange, a reddish-orange. Likewise if more yellow were added, and less red, the color produced would be yellow-orange.

Intermediate Hues are all the other hues produced in the same manner as tertiary colors, however, they fall, not halfway between primary and secondary colors on the color wheel, but only somewhere between them. An example is a blue-blue-green when more blue is added to a blue-green.

Value of Hue

Value refers to the lightness, or darkness of a hue. By adding white to a hue, it is lightened. This lightened hue is called a "tint." By adding black, or brown, it is darkened. This darkened hue is called a shade. All hues can be tinted or shaded, including primary, secondary, tertiary, and all variations of these pure hues.

Intensity of Hue

Pure colors are bright. The purity of the color determines its intensity. A pure hue is most intense, however, it is toned down by mixing it with its complement and neutralizing the hue. The result is a *muted* hue.

Pure colors are considered saturated, while muted colors are low in saturation. Pure colors have a high chroma, while muted colors have a low chroma.

COLOR WHEEL

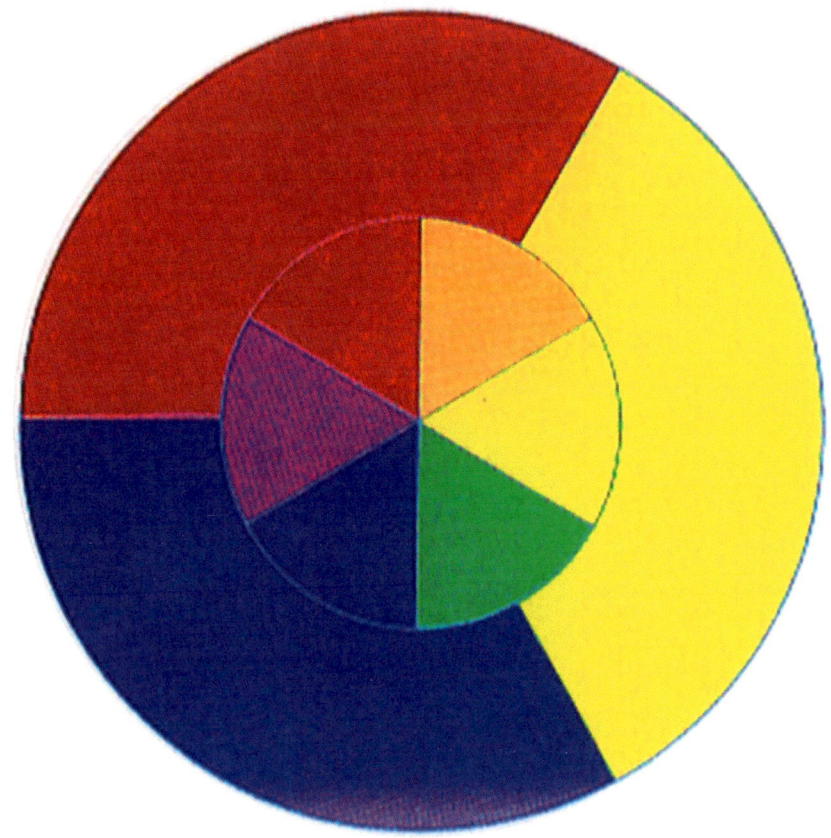

There are three **Primary Hues**, red, yellow, and blue, from which all other colors are produced. Mix red with yellow to produce orange. Mix blue with yellow to produce green. Mix red with blue to produce violet. Orange, green, and violet are **Secondary Hues**. When the three primary hues and three secondary hues are combined in a circle, these six hues form a basic **Color Wheel**.

EXTENDED COLOR WHEEL

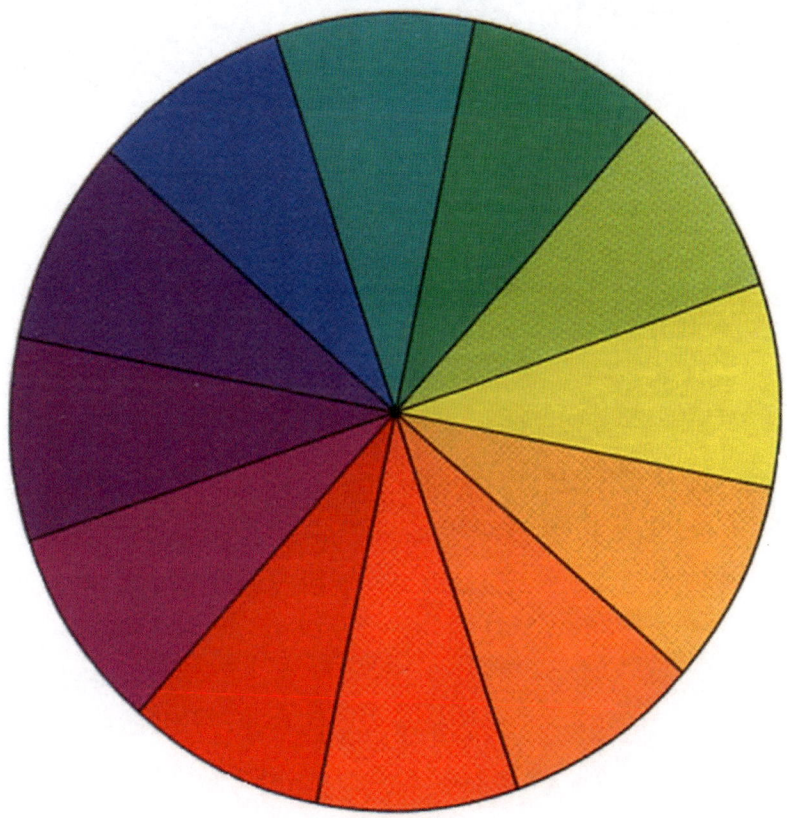

When a primary hue is mixed with a secondary hue, the result is a *Tertiary Hue.* For instance, when primary red is mixed with the secondary hue of orange, the tertiary hue of red-orange is produced. If primary yellow is added to the secondary hue of orange, the tertiary hue of yellow-orange is produced. Tertiary hues are produced <u>halfway</u> between a primary and a secondary hue.

The **Extended Color Wheel** is formed by combining the three *Primary Hues*, three *Secondary Hues*, and six *Tertiary Hues* into a color wheel.

Mix blue with yellow to you produce green. Mix red with blue to produce violet. These six hues, when put into a circle, form a *Color Wheel*.

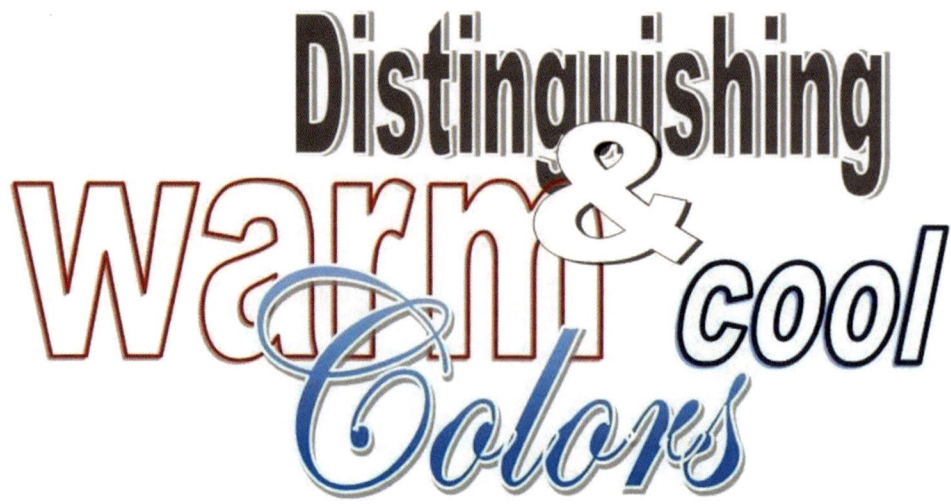

Distinguishing Warm & Cool Colors

Warm and Cool Colors of the Color Wheel

When designing with color, the first step is to decide what mood you want to adhere to. You have three choices, warm, cool, and neutral.

Warm and cool colors are colors associated with warmth and cold in nature such as the hot red or yellow sun or the cold blue running water.

Refer to COLOR WHEEL. Notice that on one side of the wheel are the warm colors, red, orange, and yellow, while the other side exhibits cool colors, green, blue, and violet.

Although pure red, yellow, and orange are equally warm colors, their derivatives may lean toward a cool spectrum. For example, a yellow that contains some blue will be "cooled" down by the blue. A red that contains some blue will also be cooled down.

The same is true of cool colors. Pure blue and green are cool colors, however, violet (purple) is derived from mixing blue, a cool color, and red, a warm color. Violet can be either a warm or cool color, depending on how it is mixed. If it is mixed with more red, it will become a warm color to be used in a warm color palette, however, if it is mixed with more blue, it will fit a cool palette.

Gray Hues

Gray is considered neutral, neither warm nor cool, however, when mixed with hues from the warm side of the color wheel, a gray becomes warmer than when mixed with a hue from the cool side. Generally, however, gray tends to add a cool mood to a room.

Warm and Cool Tints and Shades

When you change a color's value by adding neutrals such as white or black, or by adding brown, you affect the mood of the color.

Although white has a cooling affect associated with the snow of winter, it will become a "warm white" when mixed with small amounts of warm color. Similarly, a "cool white" is the result of a tint using a cool color in the tint. For example, a pink is warmer than a blue-white.

Adding black or brown to a hue will also change the warmth or coolness of the hue. Black and brown are considered warm colors because they absorb heat. When mixed with a hue, they cause the hue to "warm up."

Warm and Cool Muted Hues

Muting a pure warm color by adding its compliment will "cool down" the hue. However, there are degrees of coolness to be distinguished. The more compliment added, the cooler the result.

Muting a cool color by adding its compliment will "warm up" the hue. The more the color is muted, the warmer it will become.

Warm and Cool Textured Color

Color is affected by the material in which it is contained. A color will look different depending on the texture of the material.

A smooth, shiny surface, such as that of walls and hard-surfaced furnishings, will reflect light, therefore the color applied to it will appear *cooler*.

However, a rough-texture surface, such as that of an upholstered sofa or chair, drapery fabric, carpet, etc., absorbs light and heat, and therefore appears warmer than the same color on a smooth surface.

North and South Facing Rooms

In general, you will want to use warm colors in cool climates and cool colors in warm climates. However, this may or may not be your preference.

When choosing a color scheme for a particular room, the room's location will need to be considered. A north-facing room, which never receives direct sunlight, can be warmed up with a warm color palette, while

a south-facing room can be cooled down with a cool palette. However, if the room receiving great amounts of direct sunlight is in a northern climate, it may be preferable to enhance the warmth of this sun-lit room with a warm color palette. Similarly, if the north-facing room is in a hot southern climate, keeping it cool with a cool color palette may be the preferred choice.

Another aspect of a northerly room's location to be considered when choosing a room's colors, is that only reflected (cool) light enters a north-facing room. This reflected light has a bluish cast that will affect color in the room. It is wise to avoid the use of blue in such a room.

Warm & Cool Color Schemes

To design a room around a warm color scheme, you will want to use warm colors in your palette. To design a cool color scheme, you will want to employ cool colors. You have learned techniques to obtain warm and cool hues, now you will learn how to apply them in a color scheme.

As you have learned, red, yellow, and orange are warm colors. You have learned that adding black or brown to the mix adds warmth to the color. Colors with black and brown added are referred to as "Earth tones" because they remind us of the colors of earth's soil. Red-browns and orange-browns, referred to as "rusts," are part of the Earth tone palette.

In a warm color scheme, you will want to avoid the use of cooled down red and yellow hues, and instead incorporate warmer derivatives of these hues. You will also consider texture and the affects of color upon texture.

In a cool color scheme you will employ blues, greens, and violets and their cooled-down derivatives, also keeping in mind affects of texture.

The Color Palette

When putting a color scheme together for a room, you will need to choose a **Color Palette** that is consistent with the mood of the design. If you have decided to create a warm mood, you will choose a warm color palette. If you have decided to create a cool mood, you will use colors from the cool spectrum.

A color palette consists of a group of related colors that will work well together to accomplish your goal for the color scheme of the room. To begin to put this palette together, you will need to choose a predominant color for the scheme, that is, a color from which the scheme will be built.

Next, one, two, or three other co-ordinating colors, used in lesser amounts

Neutrals of either black, gray, white, or those of the brown spectrum, including beiges, can be added to any color scheme apart from the color palette as they do not affect mood.

Monochromatic Color Palette

In a **Monochromatic Color Palette**, only one hue is used and becomes the predominant, as well as accent, color. This hue need not be a "pure" hue, however, the scheme is built around this color by using differing values, tints, or tones of this one hue, as well as incorporating co-ordinating textures in this hue into the scheme.

Whatever the color choice for a monochromatic scheme, great care needs to be taken to use variations of the same <u>hue</u> to make the scheme work, otherwise the color will be "off." When working with a muted yellow scheme, for instance, all the colors used in the room will be those derived from that exact muted yellow. Lighter tints or darker shades will be derived from your muted color sample.

Often used in a monochromatic color scheme are neutral colors, those of white, black, or brown. In a warm white scheme, "warm whites" will be used, and in a cool scheme, "cool whites" will be used to keep the mood consistent. Similarly, a warm brown or gray room will warrant warm variations of these neutrals leaning toward the warm side of the color wheel while a cool mood will incorporate variations of these hues from the cool spectrum.

Interior Design
For Today

Adjacent Color Palette

An **Adjacent Color Palette** is referred to as an analogous color palette because colors chosen for the palette are side-by side-on the color wheel. Red and orange are adjacent to each other, therefore they can be used to produce a two-color palette. Red, red-orange, and yellow are adjacent to each other and can be used to produce a three-color palette. One of these three colors will be the predominant color and the other two will be accent colors.

When choosing a predominant color for your adjacent color scheme, keep in mind that this color is not restricted to the primary, secondary, or tertiary hues, but extended to intermediate hues as well that fall in between these on the color wheel.

Green & White Cotton Duck Print
Yellow/Green Cotton Chintz Stripe,
& Gr/Blue PlaidPercale

Complementary Color Palette

Complementary colors are colors that are opposite each other on the Color Wheel. Red and green are complimentary, blue and orange, and yellow and violet (purple). Likewise, on an extended wheel that includes tertiary colors, opposites are complementary. Blue-green is complementary to red-orange, and blue-violet is complimentary to yellow-orange, and yellow-green to red violet. If the color wheel was extended further into intermediate colors, the same theory would apply and opposites on the wheel would compliment each other.

A **_Complementary Color Palette_** is one that is built around two opposite colors on the color wheel and the scheme will use a two-color palette.

Complementary colors are opposite in mood and cancel each other out. For example, the warmth of orange is cancelled out by the coolness of blue. In order to establish a mood, one of the colors will be used as the predominant color in the scheme and the other as the accent. A cool mood, therefore, can be produced by using the blue as the predominant color in this palette and orange as the accent. A warm scheme can be achieved by using the orange as the predominant color and blue as the accent color.

Using bold bright color in a complementary color scheme produces a nervous, intense atmosphere. In order to produce a more serene, relaxed atmosphere, use either tints of both hues, or shades of both hues in equal intensity. Do not mix tinted hues with shaded hues in a palette. Similarly, combining equally muted tones of both colors will produce a pleasing palette, while a using a muted tone with an intense color will not work.

Red/Gold Flowered Taffeta, Gold Stripe Cut Velvet, & Beige Print Sailcloth

Accent Color

Optional Wall Colors

Interior Design *For Today*

Triadic Color Palette

In order to form a **_Triadic Color Palette_**, colors are chosen from those that form a triangle when the color wheel is split into thirds. A first color is chosen for the palette. The two colors at equal distance from each other in the triangle will be the other two colors of the palette.

A **_Tetradic Color Palette_** is built around four equally-distanced colors on the color wheel when the wheel is cut in quarters. In both the triadic and tetradic schemes, one color will be the dominant color in the palette while the other three colors will be distributed throughout the room in smaller amounts.

Red and purple stripe Satin weave,
Yellow twill-weave gabardine, Gold rib Satin,
Lt. beige textured waffle-weave

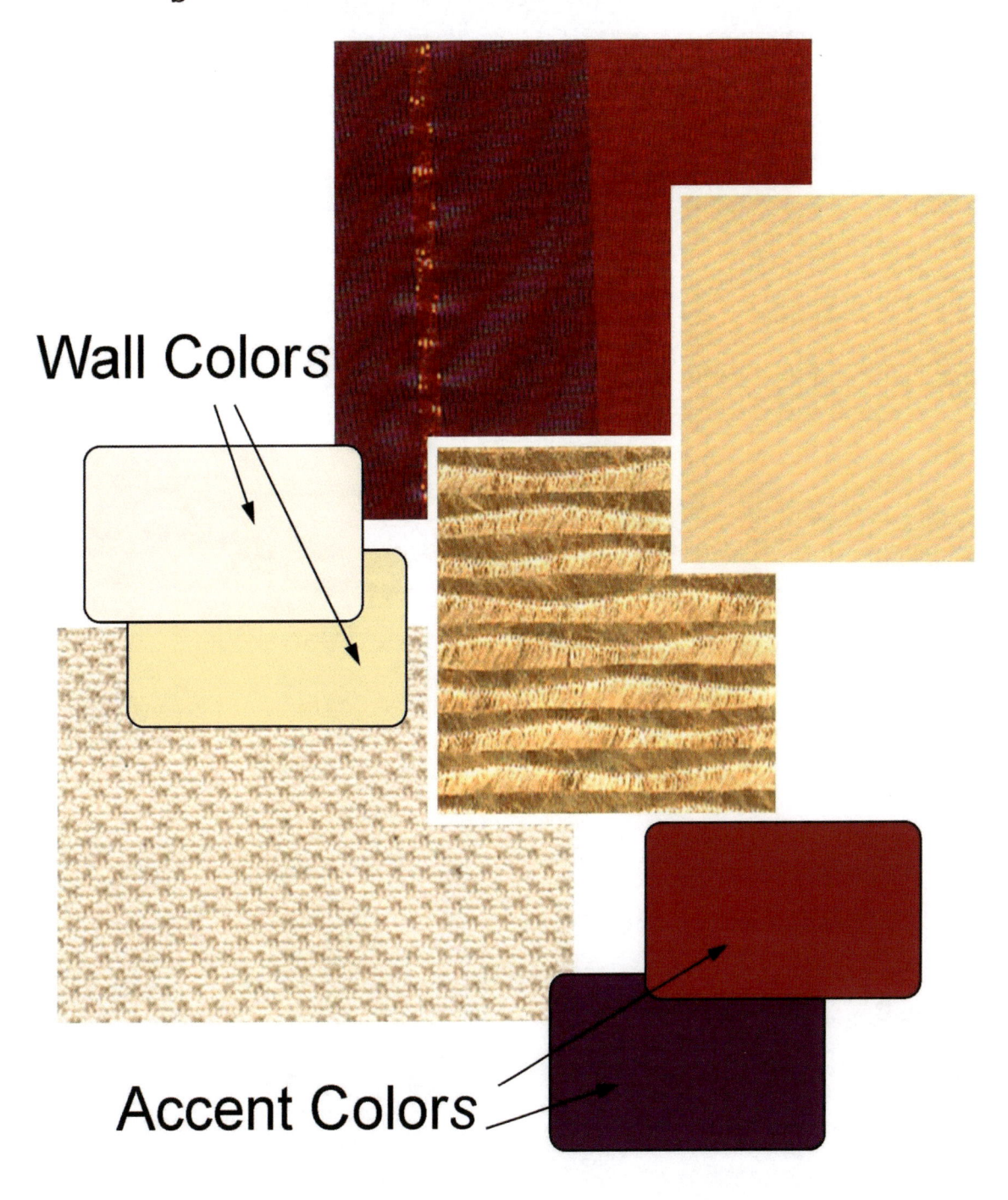

Wall Colors

Accent Colors

Interior Design
For Today

Tetradic Color Palette

A ***Tetradic Color Palette*** is built around four equally-distanced colors on the color wheel when the wheel is cut in quarters. In both the triadic and tetradic schemes, one color will be the dominant color in the palette while the other three colors will be distributed throughout the room in smaller amounts.

Mauve cotton seersucker, Yellow pin-stripe cotton

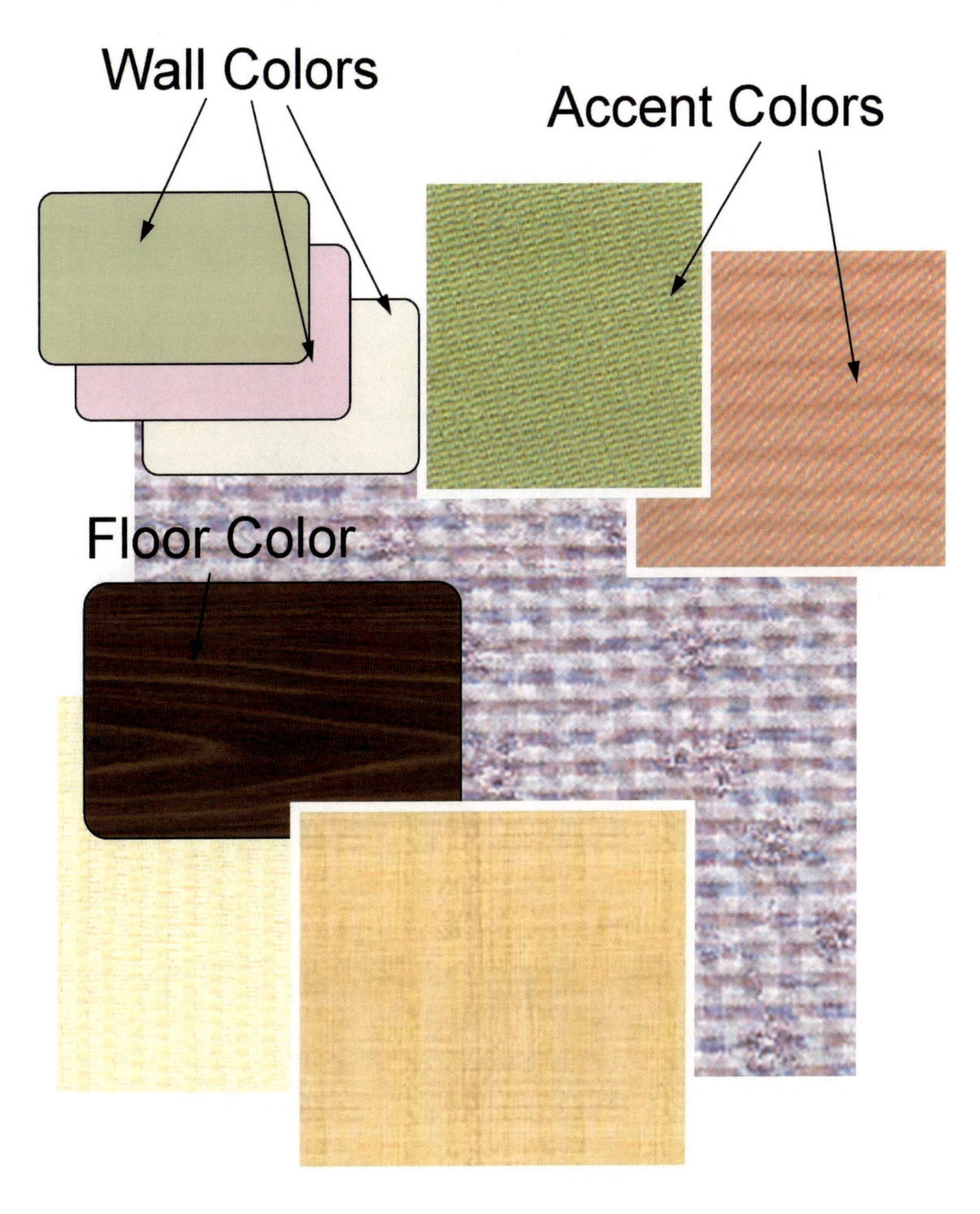

Wall Colors

Accent Colors

Floor Color

Decorating With White & The White Color Palette

Although white has been considered a non-color, a successful decorating scheme can be built around white. Just as a Monochromatic color scheme highlights the use of one color only in its palette, a **White Color Palette** focuses in on white as its predominant color. Unlike the Monochromatic scheme, however, the white color scheme takes on three different slants.

One variation of the white scheme is to use only warm whites throughout the room in varying hues. Tone-on-tone whites are added in textured fabrics used on furniture, draperies, and pillows. Silver metals, glass, and creamy ceramics complete the scheme.

A second variation of the all-white scheme is to keep the color palette white as above, but to add more warmth with a warm-wood floor and interjecting shots of bright color through accents in one additional color.

A third variation to the white palette, is to add even more warmth with natural wood, cork, linens, cottons, and wools, as well as with wooden lamps, frames, and accessories.

Choosing A Color Scheme

Generally, adjacent color schemes will be used when a very definite mood is to be produced. By using adjacent warm colors a very definite warm scheme is the result. Using adjacent cool colors will produce a definite cool scheme. If there is no definite preference, the complimentary scheme will give the benefit of creating the mood you want, either warm or cool, with less distinction because of colors counterbalancing themselves out. A monochromatic scheme presents a dramatic effect, however, tends toward boredom and will only be chosen sparingly. Once the decision is made regarding the type of scheme you want to use, the easiest way to pick a color palette is by using a color-combination that already exists in a fabric. Look for a fabric with a multi-colored pattern in the color mood you have chosen and examine it in the actual room being designed in order to see its true colors. The color combination will either fit an adjacent or complimentary scheme.

Another way to obtain an instant color palette is to look at magazine pictures and pick one in the color scheme you are most attracted to. Once you have the picture, your next step is to translate what you see into distinct colors for your palette.

Color Considerations

Variables

There are variables that affect color, including lighting, and undertone. These need to be taken into consideration when choosing color for a room.

Lighting

Color is affected by light. When choosing a color palette, always make sure to view your color choices in the room where they will be applied, as lighting in this room will be different than in the paint store from where your paint chips have come.

The less daylight entering a room, the lighter and brighter should be the color choice. In a room that receives a lot of natural light, darker values of color can be used to counteract excessive brightness. Twilight also affects color in that lighter wall colors will appear darker, while darker colors will appear lighter. Take these affects into consideration when deciding on the intensity of color to be used.

Natural light will affect a paint color differently than artificial light, and incandescent lighting will affect color differently than halogen. Incandescent lighting sheds a warm light enhancing reds, yellows, and oranges, while halogen lighting produces a cooler, blue light which enhances blues and greens, but muddies warm colors. If the fixture itself has a tinted glass, it will cast the glass's color into the room and onto the walls, and a warm-colored lamp shade will cast a warm glow.

Color in directly south-facing rooms will be affected by the warmth of natural sunlight, but a north-facing room will pick up bluish tones from reflected natural light.

COOL COLOR PALETTE

White, dark blue, light blue, grey...

Wall Colors

WARM COLOR PALETTE

Red, orange, tan, beige....

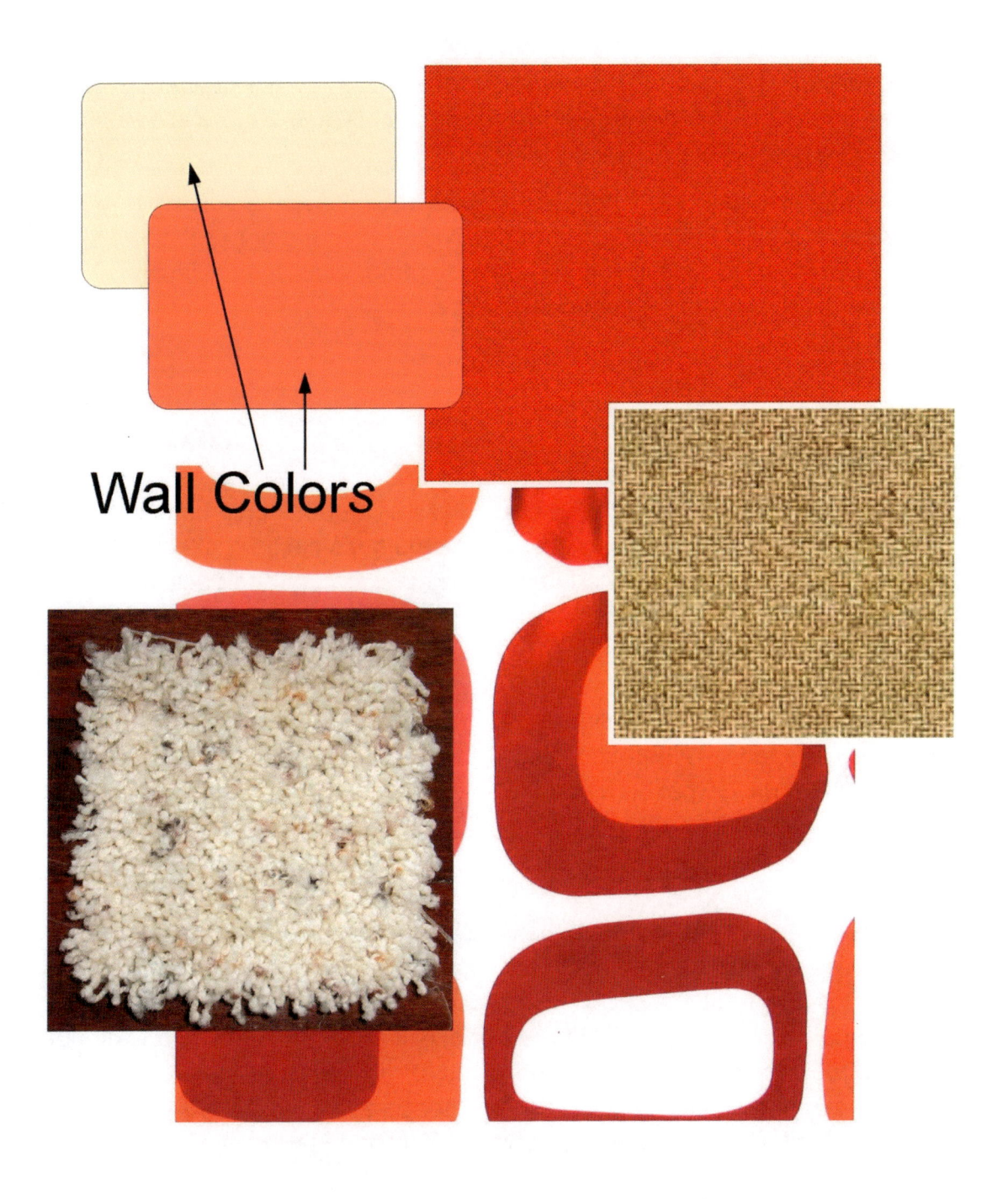

Wall Colors

Another variable to consider when putting together a color scheme, is the way light is reflected off of different surfaces in the room. You have already learned that shiny surfaces reflect light and cause the color to appear cooler, while textured surfaces absorb light and heat and cause its color to appear warmer. Light also affects color in another way when applied to a shiny surface. The color becomes more intense, while the same color applied to a textured fabric will appear dull. This information comes into play when considering visually expanding a room. Low-intensity colors make a room seem larger, while more intense colors make a space feel more closed in. If you are aiming to expand the visual size of a room, you will want wall surfaces to be painted in a flat paint and will choose furnishings with a matte finish instead of gloss.

Low-intensity cool colors tend to make a room seem larger, while warm colors bring coziness and a sense of smallness, If your color preferences fall toward warm colors, choosing a warm scheme over a cool scheme will outweigh the "closing-in" affect of warm color.

Undertones

Another consideration when choosing color, is to be aware of "undertones." Undertones are those tones that a color takes on from its original hue before being tinted, shaded, or muted. You have already studied the effects altering color by changing its value and intensity and of warming and cooling it. You have also learned that altered colors stem from an original "pure hue." Undertones are the tones of the pure hue a color was originally mixed from. For example, pure red has no undertone because it is a primary color. However, when mixed with yellow it becomes orange. Orange, therefore, has a yellow undertone. When choosing pre-mixed color, you will not have the privilege of knowing what pure hue it was derived from. You will need to train your eye to detect undertones. By examining the color, you will be able to tell if the undertones are reddish, yellowish, or bluish. Yellow with a blue undertone will look green when applied to a wall. The blue undertones affect the color, and different forms of lighting in a room will cause its affect to be emphasized even more. For example, gray, with a warm red undertone will look cooler under fluorescent or halogen lighting than sunlight. It is of great importance to determine what the undertone is so that the scheme will not clash. Choose colors with warm undertones for a warm palette, and with cool undertones for a cool palette. When choosing wall color to "work" with patterned fabrics, analyze the background color for undertones and apply wall color with similar undertones.

Pay Attention to Undertones

Designing with Fabric

When designing with fabric, it is important to understand how fabrics are de rived. Some are produced from **Natural Fibers** such as **Cotton**, **Wool,** and **Silk**. Others are produced from synthetically made fibers. These, as well as an array of mixed fibers, are woven together to produce fabrics suitable for home interior use. We will briefly cover the main fabrics and blends in this lesson, learning of their fiber content and **weave**.

Fabric Fibers

Natural Fibers

Cotton is a strong fabric when "mercerized," that is, when treated chemically to toughen its limp natural plant fiber. Cotton can be spun to varying degrees of tightness, making the fabric stronger the more-tightly its yarn is spun. It reflects light and heat and is considered a cool warm-weather fabric.

Cotton fabrics are not considered luxurious and have the added disadvantage of wrinkling, however, when blended with synthetic fibers, which are man-made, these negatives are limited.

Wool is an animal fiber. It is durable, soft, wrinkle-free, colorfast, and fade-resistant, and can be treated for moth and dirt resistance. Wool is considered a luxury fabric.

Another natural fabric is that of **Linen** which is made from flax plant fibers. Linen has a firm, crisp, textured look and feel. It, as cotton, reflects heat and is considered a "cool" fabric in warm weather. One disadvantage to linen is that it is not wrinkle-free and therefore is best when interwoven with wrinkle-free synthetics. Another drawback of linen is that it does not take dye well and color choices are restricted.

Silk is produced by the silk worm and considered a very luxurious fabric. It is soft, sheer, delicate fabric fabric that is very durable. It takes color well, and when dyed, the color is vibrant. Silk however, has the drawback of staining easily and fading in light.

Synthetic Fibers

Acrylic, **Nylon**, **Polyester**, **polyamide, polypropylene**, **Acetate**, **Viscose**,and **Rayon** are all man-made synthetic fibers. They have the benefits of durability, resilience, and they take dyes well. Although they have some drawbacks, when used in the right blend with cotton or wool, they produce fabrics which can be fine, medium, or upholstery weighted. All these fabrics can be treated to protect from stains and flames with stain-resistant and flame-retardant products.

Fiber Blends

In decorating today, a variety of new and improved blended fabrics with improved yarns and fashion sense are available. Machine-embroidered and appliqued embellishments are added as well as metallic yarns to give shimmer and shine. Heavily textured and quilted fabrics bring drama. Graphically embossed velvets are available in bright, rich new color for freshness. These fabrics are available in various blends of Cotton/Linen, Polyester/Silk, Polyester/Rayon, Acetate/Silk, Cotton/Silk/Acrylic, Rayon/Polyester, Wool/Cotton, Acetate/Nylon, Viscose/Silk, Viscose/Cotton, Polyester/Cotton/Viscose, Acrylic/Polyester/Cotton, Viscose/ Polyamide/Polypropylene, and the list goes on. Many hard-wearing appropriate fabrics have "unknown" fiber content. Though these may be less preferred, they are still an option if the color, pattern design, weight, and quality are right for the job.

Fabric Weaves

Plain Weave

Plain weave is a simple criss-cross patterned weave, which, when woven with fine threads, produces a **Taffeta** weave, and when woven with thicker threads to produce more texture, a **Basket** weave.

Cotton can be plain-woven into various light-weight fabrics including *Gauze* and plain un-dyed *Muslin,* as well as *Organdy* and *Voile* which are treated with stiffener and dyed in a variety of colors. These fabrics are used for fine draperies.

Cotton *Gingham* is a lightweight weave of two colored yarns producing squares, checks, or stripes. It is used for bedcovers, curtains, and draperies.

Percale, which is a heavier grade of plain-weave cotton with varying thread counts from 180 up to 600, is used for sheeting.

Canvas, a heavier, coarser version of plain-woven cotton, is used for awnings, casual exterior upholstery, and for slip-covers. Less coarse versions of canvas include *Duck Cloth* and *Sail Cloth* which can be used for interior upholstery, pillow covers, and slip-covers, *Ticking* is another variation which is a striped fabric reserved for pillow casings.

Chintz is a finely plain-woven cotton that is glazed for dirt-resistance and stiffening which produces a shiny surface. Chintz fabrics come in either solids or colored prints. Chinz is used for draperies, upholstery, pillow covers, and slip-covers.

Chiffon is a light-weight plain-weave sheer fabric in silk, wool, or synthetic fiber used for sheer curtains.

Satin Weave

When fabrics are woven with a **Satin Weave**, the surface of the fabric is smooth and shiny, while the back is dull. Silks and synthetics can be woven in this manner. When cotton is woven in this fashion, it is referred to as **Sateen**.

Fine satins are used for sheets, draperies, and pillow covers. Because of cotton's ability to fade in the sun, cotton sateen is restricted to bed covers and pillow covers, and is not recommended for draperies.

Twill Weave

Twill weaves feature threads in a diagonal pattern. *Gabardine* and *Serge* are tightly woven twill weaves with a hard, resilient surface. They are suitable for upholstery. Cotton *denim* is also a twill-weave fabric used for upholstery, pillow covers, and bedding.

Pile Weave

Pile-woven fabrics are woven with loops that are either cut or left uncut to form texture. *Terrycloth* is manufactured with uncut loops to produce a loose pile weave with a highly textured surface. It is used for upholstering in wet areas. *Velvet* is pile-woven with cut loops to form a smooth surface. When varying lengths of pile loops are cut to form a pattern, the fabric is referred to as *cut velvet*, when crushed, *crushed velvet*. Velvet is a heavy fabric used for upholstery, bedding, pillow covers, and draperies of rich opulence.

Alternate rows of low-level and high-level cut loops form *Corduroy*. Corduroy can be of light weight, medium weight, or heavy weight, usually in cotton and is used for pillow covers, bedding, and much less for upholstery because of cotton's tendency to stretch out of shape.

Jacquard Weave

Jacquard weaves are fabrics with complex pattern woven into them. *Brocade* is a heavy fabric with a contrasting raised Jacquard design and used for draperies. *Damask* is also a fabric with a raised woven-in jacquard pattern, but it is light-weight and reversible, often used for table linens. Medium to heavy-weight *Jacquards*, using blended fibers, are used for draperies, pillow covers, and especially for upholstery.

The Fabric Palette

In implementing a color scheme in a room, a first step is to put together a **Fabric Palette** by choosing fabrics for the main items in the room, including soft furnishings such as *sofas, upholstered chairs*, and *draperies*. Accent fabrics for pillow covers, throws, and bedding, will then be added to the palette.

When choosing fabrics, keep in mind texture and incorporate textured fabrics that enhance the mood and style of the room. In a traditional scheme, satin, velvet, and silk are appropriate, while in a more contemporary scheme, leather, corduroy, faux suede, faux fur, wool, and silk-look fabrics are appropriate. Adding a variety of rough and smooth textured fabrics add interest.

Study the following GATHERING FABRIC SAMPLES A, B, C, and D helps. Study them to learn how to put a fabric palette together with fabrics of appropriate weight for their use. Observe the weave and detail of print and color as you proceed through this lesson. When you are finished this lesson, you will be equipped to visit a fabric store and choose upholstery, drapery, bed, and accessory fabrics for your palette.

Upholstery Fabrics

Fabrics being selected need to suit their function. Fabric on a sofa or upholstered chair, for instance, that will be subject to wear and tear, needs to be durable. Delicate fabrics such as silk, or satin will not perform. A most durable fabric is wool, a natural fabric made from wool fiber. However, wool is exceptionally expensive, and nylon, which is a man-made fiber is equally strong and resilient. Nylon has added advantages in that it repels mildew and moths, it is washable, and it does not stretch out of shape. Nylon and nylon-blends in a heavy upholstery-weight fabric are a good upholstery choice.

Brown Heavy Jacquard

& Orange/White Print

Heavy Cotton

GATHERING FABRIC SAMPLES A

Dark Green Heavy Cotton Print, Beige Moire, & Sage Green Cotton/

GATHERING FABRIC SAMPLES B

Red/Green Flowered Taffeta, Red Striped Moire, & Spring Green Basket Weave Heavy Cotton

GATHERING FABRIC SAMPLES C

Black/White Sateen Floral,

Black Jacquard,

& Red Moire

GATHERING FABRIC SAMPLES D

When choosing a fabric for upholstery, take care to consult your fabric supplier regarding fade-resistance of the fabric.

Applying stain repellent protective treatments to the fabric will resist soiling. If the fabric is not pre-treated, treat it once it has been applied to a piece of furniture.

When choosing patterned upholstery fabrics, keep in mind the proportion of the patterns to the object it is covering, as well as to the size of the room. For instance, large patterns and prints work well on a big piece of furniture, in a large room. However, smaller prints suit smaller pieces of furniture and work better in a small space.

If more than one print is being used, care must be taken to co-ordinate these prints color-wise as well as scale-wise. A rule of thumb is to have no more than one bold pattern per room. A second pattern can be used, but it needs to be subtle enough that it does not compete for attention with the first pattern. A stripe fabric may be added to a palette with prints. Use of too bold or too much print or pattern in a room can be overwhelming and create confusion, therefore, choices need to be made carefully.

When putting together you palette for a Living Room, choose your sofa fabric first. If you are purchasing a ready-made sofa or club chairs, select them in the color and fabric of your choice. Take a trip to a furniture store to see and feel fabrics applied to such furnishings. Floor model styles come in various fabrics and color choices.

Because the purchase of a sofa is one of the most expensive in the room, opt for a color and fabric that is neutral so that it will "work" with any decor. However, if more flare is preferred, a more vibrant color, print, or pattern will suit.

The detail of choices in upholstery fabric will be dictated to you by the style and mood you are implementing in the room. If you are going for a more traditional palette, jacquards are a good choice. If less opulence is required, and a more refined look is needed, leather, or wool, or wool blend fabrics in a plain weave will qualify. For a more contemporary style of room, a faux suede or leather in a neutral color will suit. Refer to the following CONTEMPORARY FURNITURE STYLE furniture samples.

For a relaxed cottage style room, cottons and linens with stripes or florals are suitable upholstery fabrics.

Draperies

The second choice in putting together a palette is that of draperies. Their fabric will need to co-ordinate with upholstery fabrics in the room.

When choosing a drapery fabric, the way a fabric "drapes" when hung is of utmost importance. If the fabric is too stiff, it will not drape properly. Because draperies are lined, a variety of fabrics, from fine to heavy can be used.

Natural silk or linen are traditional choices for formal draperies, however, a less expensive application of man-made synthetic fabrics or cotton/synthetic blends are a good choice. Once again, the mood of the room will dictate color and print or stripe detail.

If ready-made draperies are to be used in the room, the choice of these will need to fit the mood and style of the room and will add a second color to the color scheme palette.

Interior Design
For Today

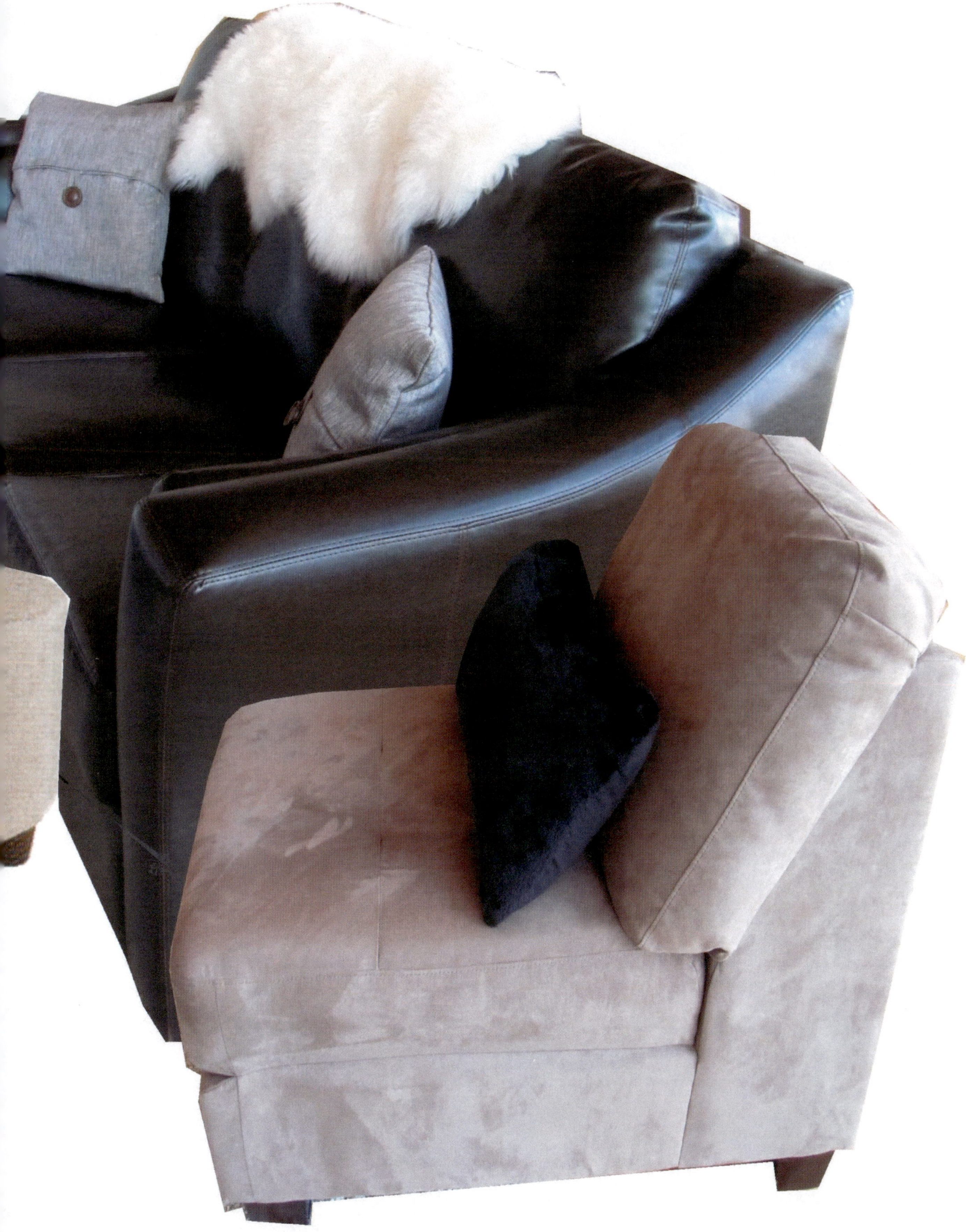

Bedding

In a bedroom, the focus of attention is on the bed, therefore bedding fabrics will be a major choice in the fabric palette along with the draperies.

Choose medium to heavyweight fabrics that are washable or dry-cleanable. Add texture with smooth silk-like fabrics, or add flare with a woven print fabric. Choice of bedding fabric will dictate the main color choice in the palette.

Rugs and Carpeting

Rugs and carpeting are fabric choices for your room. Bold patterned rugs need special consideration. If their pattern is dominant, upholsteries and draperies in the room will need to be fairly neutral so as not to compete with it. If printed or patterned fabrics for upholsteries and draperies have already been chosen, area rugs and carpeting will need to be very low-key and neutral so as not to compete with or overwhelm these fabric choices.

Completing a Color Scheme

           *U*p to this point, you have studied color and fabrics, and have learned how to put together a color palette as well as a fabric palette. In this lesson you will learn how to complete the color scheme by adding wall, accent, and floor colors to a color palette. Refer back o the samples of COLOR PALETTE, COMPLEMENTARY COLOR PALETTE, ADJACENT COLOR PALETTE, MONOCHROMATIC COLOR PALETTE, TRIADIC COLOR PALETTE, and TETRADIC COLOR PALETTE when reading this chapter.

Having already gathered fabric samples for upholstery and draperies, as well as for bedding, the color scheme palette will already have been started. The next step is to analyze your fabric color choices and decide if they fall into a monochromatic, adjacent, complementary, triadic, or tetradic scheme.

Referring to the palette of the COLOR PALETTE, blue and white are the colors of fabric, and a dark reddish-brown, the color of the floor. In order to choose a wall color that fits with this palette, two tints of the floor color have been chosen. An optional wall color choice could be a pale tint of the blue hue used in the fabrics. Adding an area rug in a tint of the brown hue will soften the hardness of the floor color.

Reddish-brown is a very muted derivative of orange. Blue and orange are opposites on the color wheel. White is a neutral. Can you guess what type of color scheme this palette falls into? If you said Complimentary, you are right.

Refer to the COMPLEMENTARY COLOR PALETTE. As can be seen, the choices of fabrics in this scheme co-ordinate color-wise. Upholsteries are in gold and beige and the drapery fabric falls into the same category of warm browns, however, the pattern brings other colors into the palette, red and green.

As you know from studying your color wheel, red and green are opposites, therefore complementary. By pulling red and green out and into the palette, a Complementary Color Scheme is the result.

Wall color choices could go light or dark, or an accent wall could be painted with the intense gold tone while the other walls are painted in the light beige tint. The important thing to remember when choosing wall colors based on fabric choices, is to determine the exact hue from which they will be derived. For instance, the darker wall color is the same hue as what is found in the printed drapery fabric, while the lighter color is a tint of the same hue. This fabric and color scheme is appropriate for a traditional setting.

Refer to the ADJACENT COLOR PALETTE . This color palette consists of fabrics chosen for a cottage scheme which include cottons in a variety of weights. Colors range from greens to blues to yellows. Looking at the Color Wheel, you will see that these colors are adjacent to each other. A medium blue, pulled from the plaid fabric, and a dark green, pulled from the print and repeated in the stripe, enhance the scheme when used for accents

The wall colors are derivatives of the yellow hue in the striped fabric.

COOL COLOR PALETTE

Blue Cotton Chintz, White Wide Wale Corduroy & Brown Print, Fine Rib Corduroy, & Dk. Blue Basket Weave Heavy Cotton

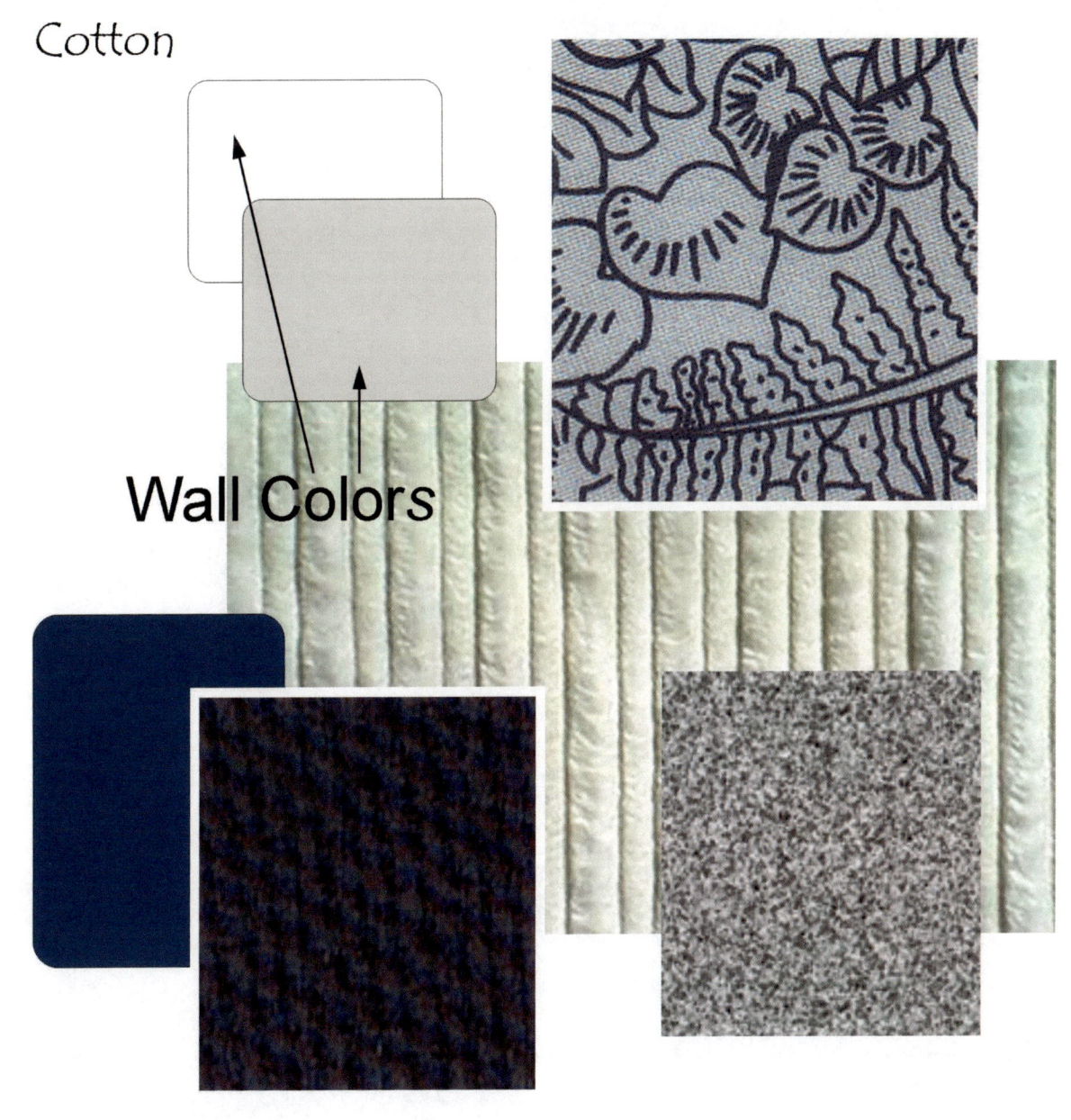

Wall Colors

Red/Gold Flowered Taffeta Draperies, Gold Stripe Cut Velvet, & Beige Print Sailcloth Upholsteries

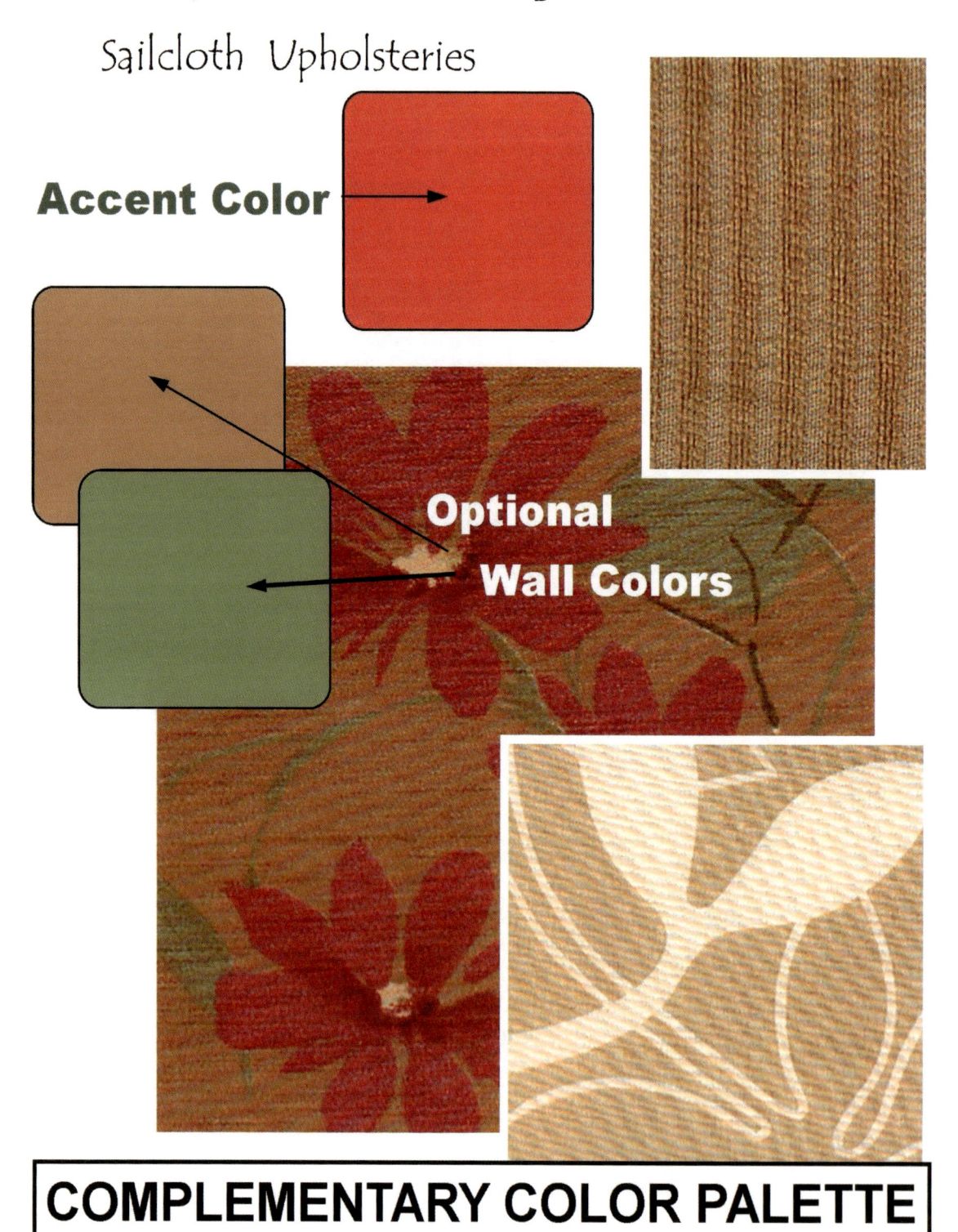

Accent Color

Optional Wall Colors

COMPLEMENTARY COLOR PALETTE

Cottage Pics

Green & White Cotton Duck Print Draperies, Yellow/Green Cotton Chintz Stripe, & Gr/Blue Plaid Percale Bedding

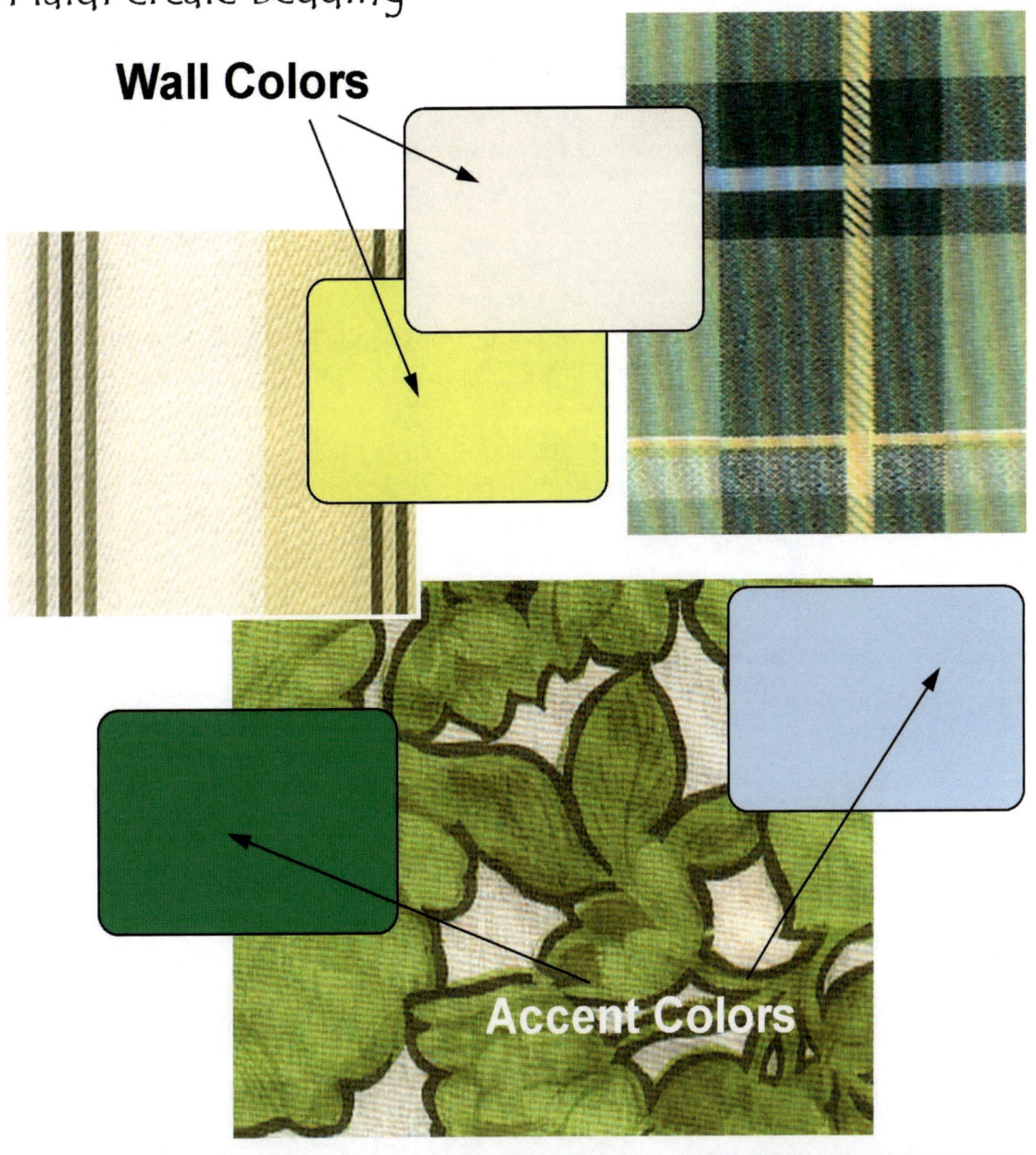

Wall Colors

Accent Colors

ADJACENT COLOR PALETTE

Refer to the MONOCHROMATIC COLOR PALETTE. As can be seen, the main color this palette is based on is brown. Upholstery and drapery fabrics are from the brown spectrum. Three of the wall color choices are derived from the brown hue of the Damask upholstery fabric, while another choice is a tint of the beige hue of the faux suede upholstery fabric. A deep rich dark brown is pulled out in accent pieces.

Refer to the TRIADIC COLOR PALETTE. This palette includes colors that are chosen from a triad of colors on the color wheel, red, purple, and gold. A light beige neutrals is added in carpeting. Wall colors in the palette include two choices of warm tinted yellows based on the yellow hue of the upholstery fabric.

Refer to the TETRADIC COLOR PALETTE. This palette draws colors from four corners of the color wheel. Mauve, a tinted derivative of violet, sage, a tinted derivative of green, a pale tinted yellow, and salmon, a tinted derivative of red-orange form this palette. Mauve cotton seersucker is used for the bedding, pale yellow cotton for draperies, and pale sage and salmon for accents. Wall color choices are further tints of these colors. A sisal area rug covers a dark red-brown hardwood floor.

Brown Heavy Damask upholstery, Faux Suede upholstery, & Brown Striped Satin Draperies

OPTIONAL WALL COLORS

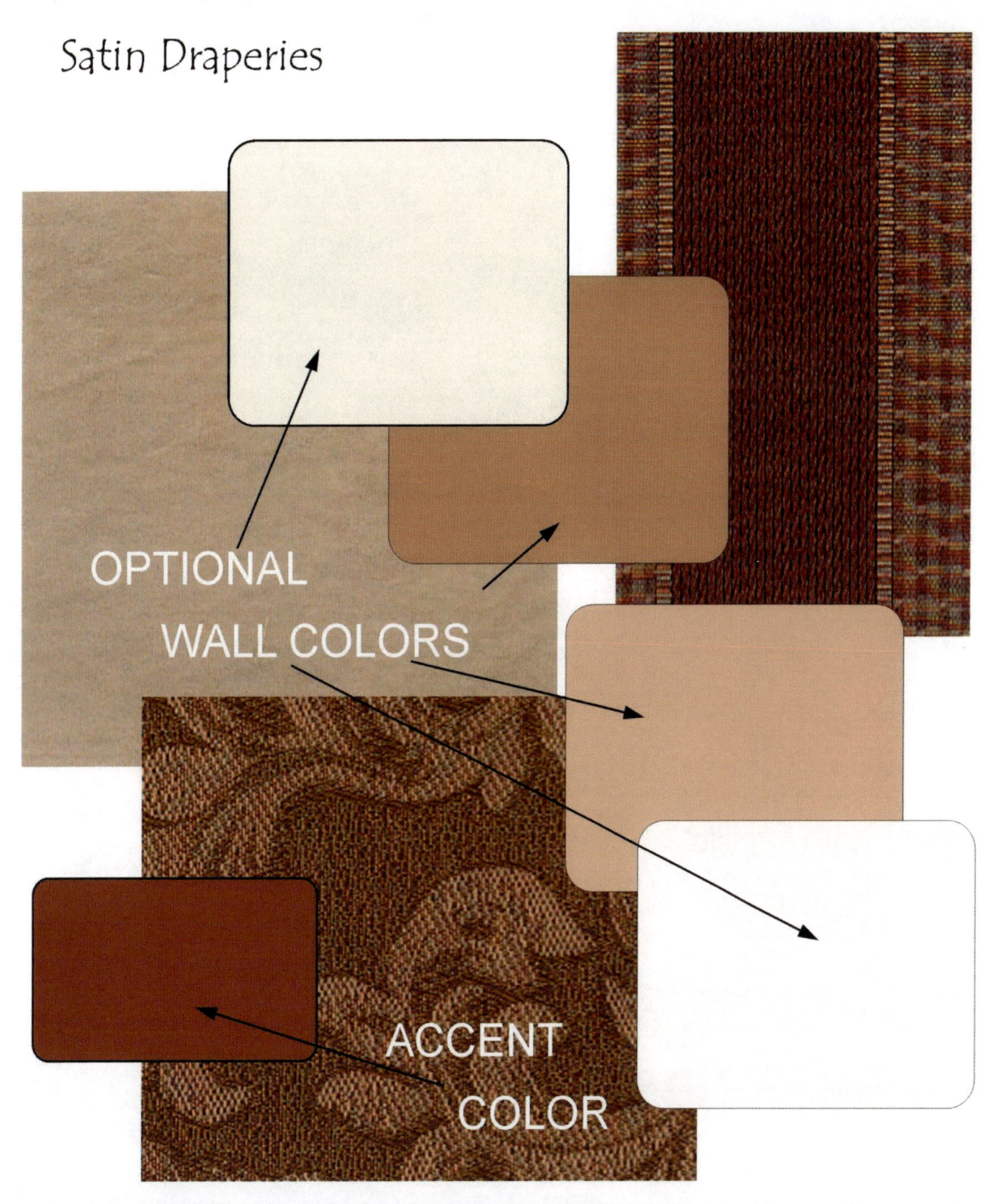

ACCENT COLOR

MONOCHROMATIC COLOR PALETTE

Interior Design
For Today

Red and purple stripe Satin weave draperies, Yellow twill-weave gabardine upholstery, Gold rib Satin bed cover, Lt. beige plush carpeting

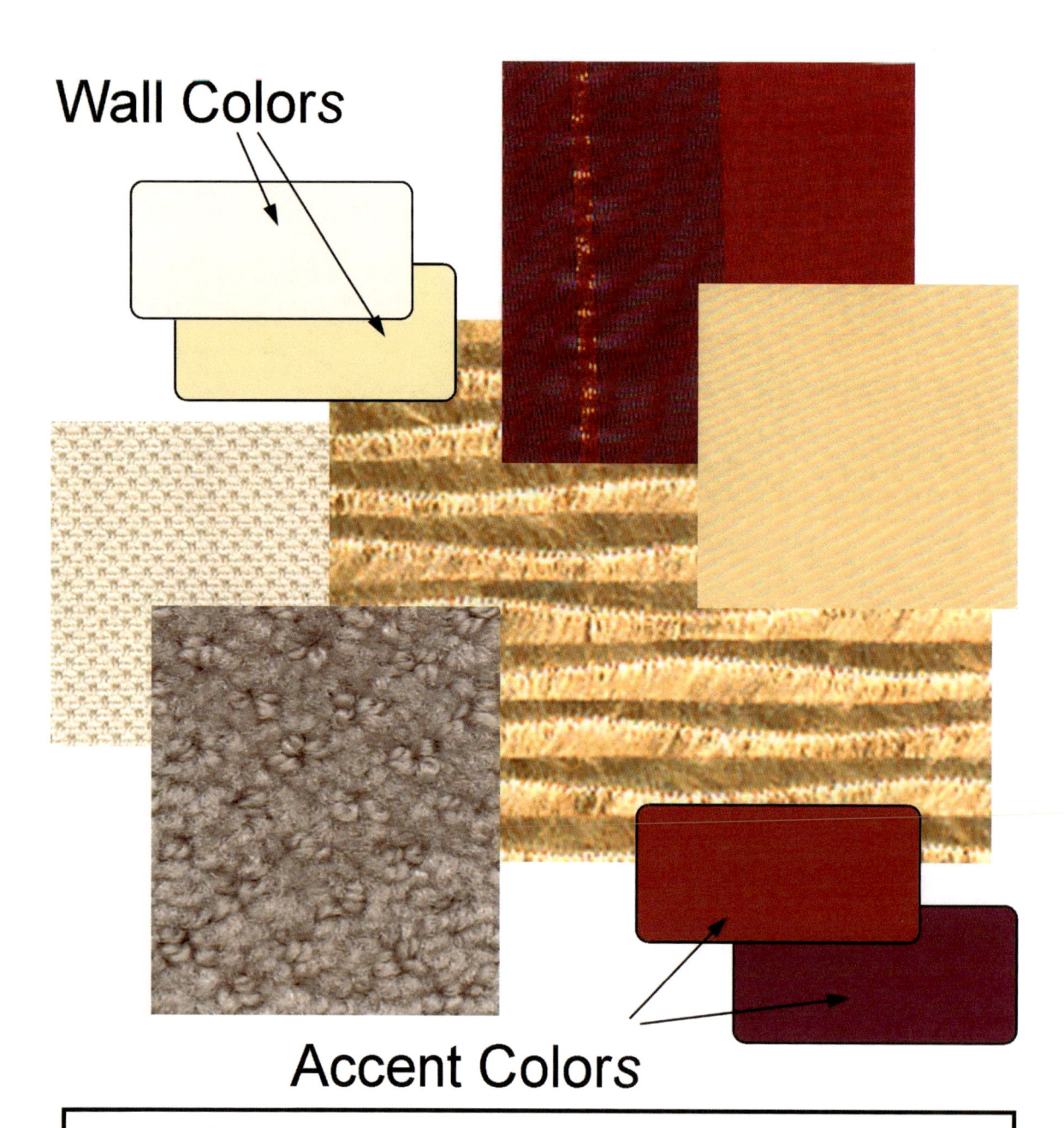

Wall Colors

Accent Colors

TRIADIC COLOR PALETTE

Mauve cotton seersucker bedding, Yellow pin-stripe cotton draperies, sisal area rug

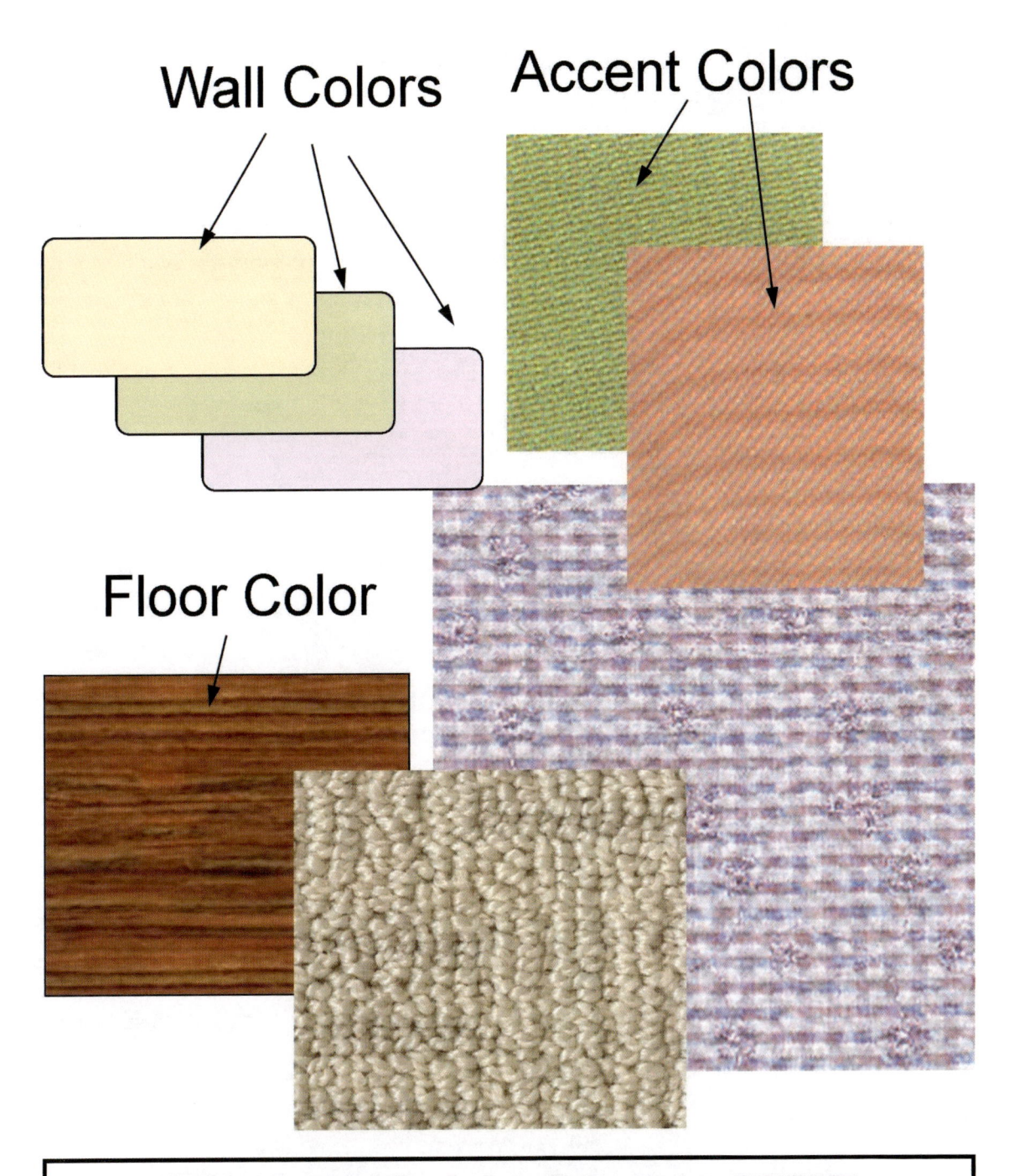

Wall Colors

Accent Colors

Floor Color

TETRADIC COLOR PALETTE

UNIT II DESIGN PROJECT Part A

The following design project will further your training and enhance your learning experience. Complete UNIT II DESIGN PROJECT Part A projects before beginning UNIT II Part B.

1. Complete a **COLOR WHEEL Practice Sheet**. Re-read the lesson on Primary & Secondary Hues and the Color Wheel and refer to the COLOR WHEEL. Use a water color paint kit to color in the primary and secondary colors. Mix equal amounts of primary color to produce secondary color. In order to keep colors from becoming muddied while mixing, clean your brush with water between applications. Practice mixing colors on your palette and test them on scrap paper before applying them to your finished presentation.

2. Complete a **COLOR WHEEL Exercise**. Re-read the lesson entitled Primary & Secondary Hues and the Color Wheel and refer to the COLOR WHEEL. Use your paint kit to mix color and apply it to the wheel using the method of practice and testing before applying.

3. Complete a **TERTIARY COLOR Exercise**. Re-read the lesson entitled Tertiary& Intermediate Hues. Mix and apply colors with preliminary practice and testing of color before applying it to your Exercise.

4. Complete a **COLOR VALUE Exercise**. Re-read the lesson on UNDERSTANDING COLOR. Paint pure hues in the boxes as indicated and tints and shades of that hue in boxes to the left and right as indicated.

5. Complete a **COLOR INTENSITY Exercise.** Paint pure hues in the boxes as indicated. Mute them slightly and paint this muted hue in the boxes indicated. Continue to mute the hue till it is extra muted and paint a sample of this muted hue in the box indicated "extra muted."

PRIMARY HUE   SECONDARY HUE

Red   *Orange*

Yellow   *Violet*

Blue   *Green*

COLOR WHEEL Practice Sheet

Interior Design For Today

COLOR WHEEL

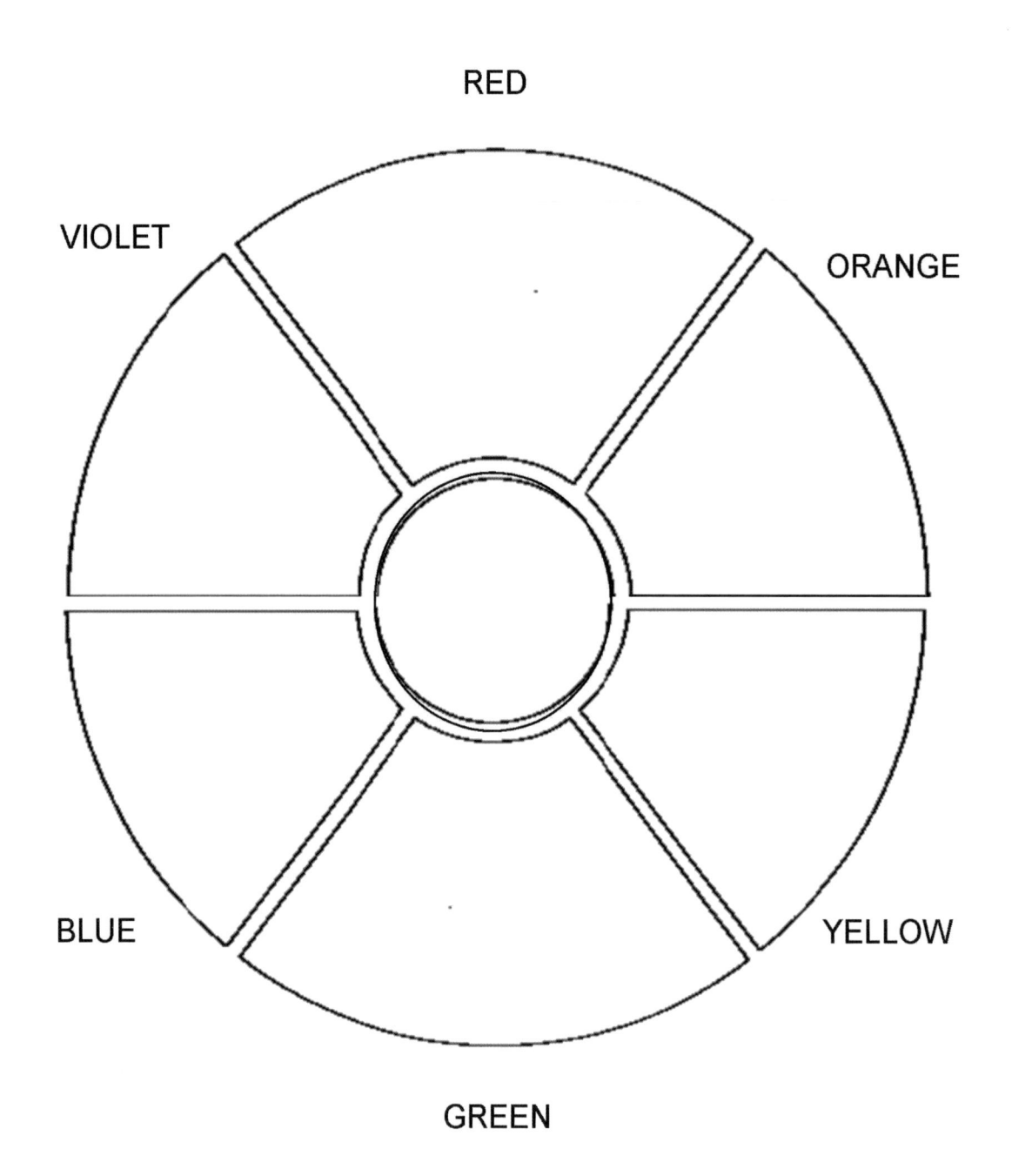

RED

VIOLET

ORANGE

BLUE

YELLOW

GREEN

COLOR WHEEL Exercise

Interior Design For Today

TERTIARY COLOR

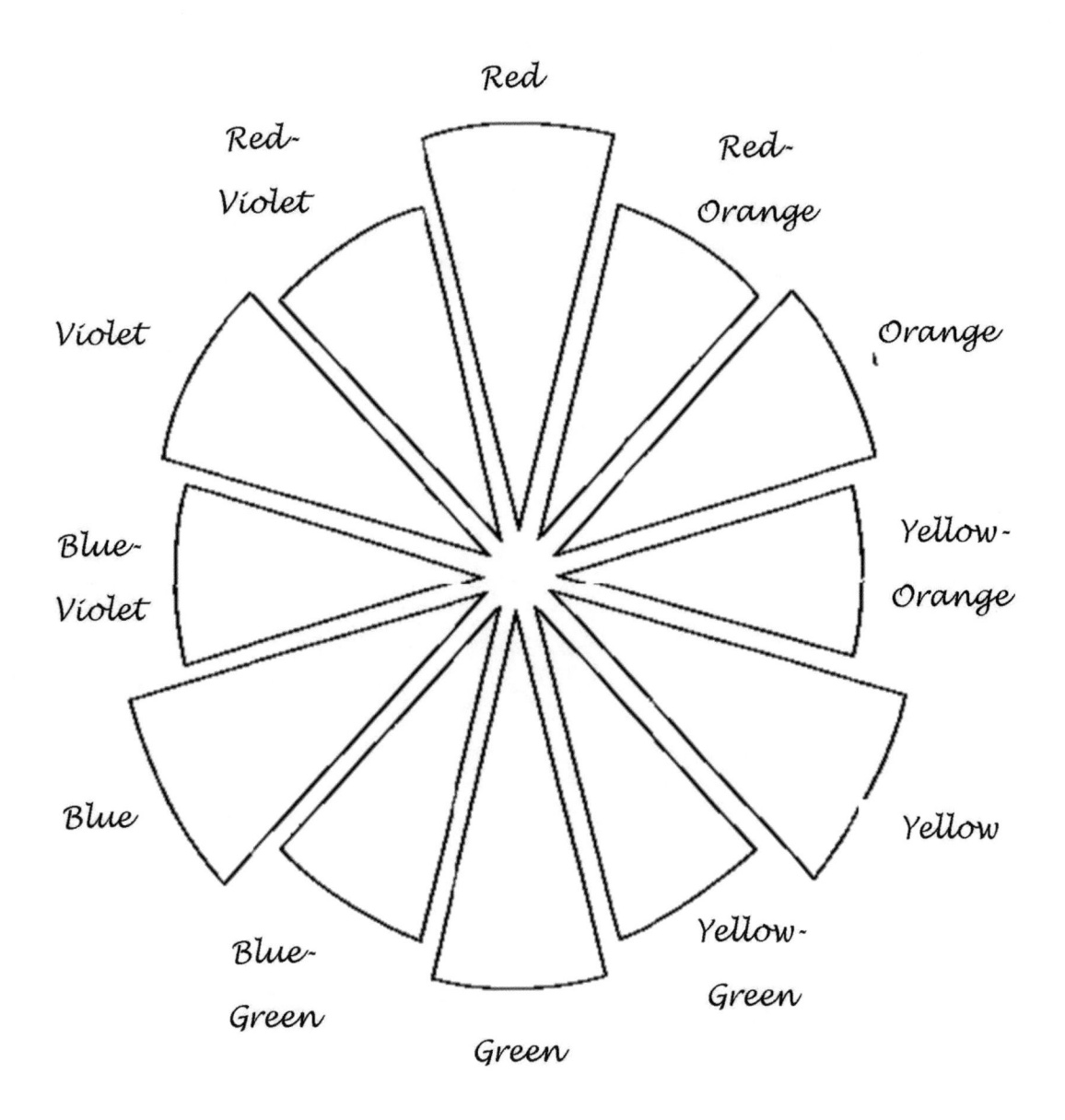

Red
Red-Violet
Red-Orange
Violet
Orange
Blue-Violet
Yellow-Orange
Blue
Yellow
Blue-Green
Yellow-Green
Green

TERTIARY COLOR Exercise

Interior Design For Today

TINT	PURE HUE	SHADE
	Red	
	Blue	
	Yellow	
	Orange	
	Green	
	Violet	

COLOR VALUE Exercise

ARMING COLORS Exercise. Re-read OOL COLORS. In the COOLING A WARM UE in the top box. In the next box down, m box, paint in its MUTED HUE. In the mn, paint in the PURE HUE. In the next d its MUTED HUE. Pre-mix and test your

7. Complete a **Color Scheme board for your Living Room, Bedroom, and Dining Room**, and for **Stafford's Living/Dining Room**. To stay within your guidelines of color, mood, and style preferences, refer to your ROOM USE QUESTIONNAIREs prepared for your Living Room and Dining room. A ROOM USE QUESTIONNAIRE for Bedroom and a ROOM USE QUESTIONNAIRE for Stafford's Living/Dining Room is supplied with your helps.

	PURE HUE	MUTED HUE	EXTRA
Red			
Green			
Blue			
Orange			
Yellow			
Violet			

COLOR INTENSITY Exercise

Interior Design For Today

COOLING A WARM COLOR	WARMING A COOL COLOR
RED	BLUE
PURE HUE	**PURE HUE**
add WHITE	add BLACK or BROWN
TINT	**SHADE**
add COMPLIMENT	add COMPLIMENT
MUTED HUE	**MUTED HUE**

COOLING & WARMING COLORS

Interior Design For Today

Choose one palette each of a Monochromatic, Adjacent, or Complementary Color Scheme for each of your rooms. Trace the following to make your own **MONOCHROMATIC COLOR SCHEME Board**, **ADJACENT COLOR SCHEME Board**, **COMPLEMENTARY COLOR SCHEME Board** and **STAFFORD'S LIVING/DINING ROOM COLOR SCHEME Board** to mount fabric samples, paint color samples, floor color samples, and accent color samples.

Gather fabric samples for upholsteries and draperies, as well as accent fabrics for each of your rooms. To do this, visit a large fabric center which supplies multiple choices in fabrics. Have the minimum allowance of each fabric choice cut for you. Take your fabric samples to a paint store and match paint samples to them based on the pure hue in the fabric sample.

Write in the name of the room. Give a brief description of fabrics and their use. Refer to your helps. To cut tidy fabric samples for your boards that won't fray, use strips of masking tape on the back sides along the edges. Apply your samples neatly with glue. These boards will form your color schemes for your rooms.

Fabric Sample Description

A. _____

B. _____

C. _____

Wall Color

Floor

A

B

C

Accent

MONOCHROMATIC COLOR

Interior Design For Today

Fabric Sample Description

A. _____

B. _____

C. _____

Wall Color

Floor

A

B

C

Accent

ADJACENT COLOR SCHEME

Fabric Sample Description

A. _____

B. _____

C. _____

Wall Color

Floor

A

B

C

Accent

COMPLIMENTARY COLOR SCHEME

Interior Design For Today

Fabric Sample Description

A. _____

B. _____

C. _____

D. _____

Wall Colors

Floor Colors

Accent Colors

A.

B.

C.

D.

STAFFORD'S LIVING/DINING ROOM COLOR SCHEME BOARD

Interior Design For Today

Designing with Window Treatments

Window Treatments add impact to the decorating scheme of a room, and choosing the right treatment for a window is of great importance. Although window treatments do cover a window, that is not their only function. They "dress" a window and work together with other elements in the room to present an aesthetically pleasing look. In other words, adding window treatments to your windows not only provide a much needed function, but contribute to the decorating scheme of the room.

In this lesson, you will be made aware of various choices in Window Treatments and learn how to successfully apply them to your decorating scheme.

Horizontal blinds

Interior Design For Today

Interior Design
For Today

Problem A: Window too short compared to its wall

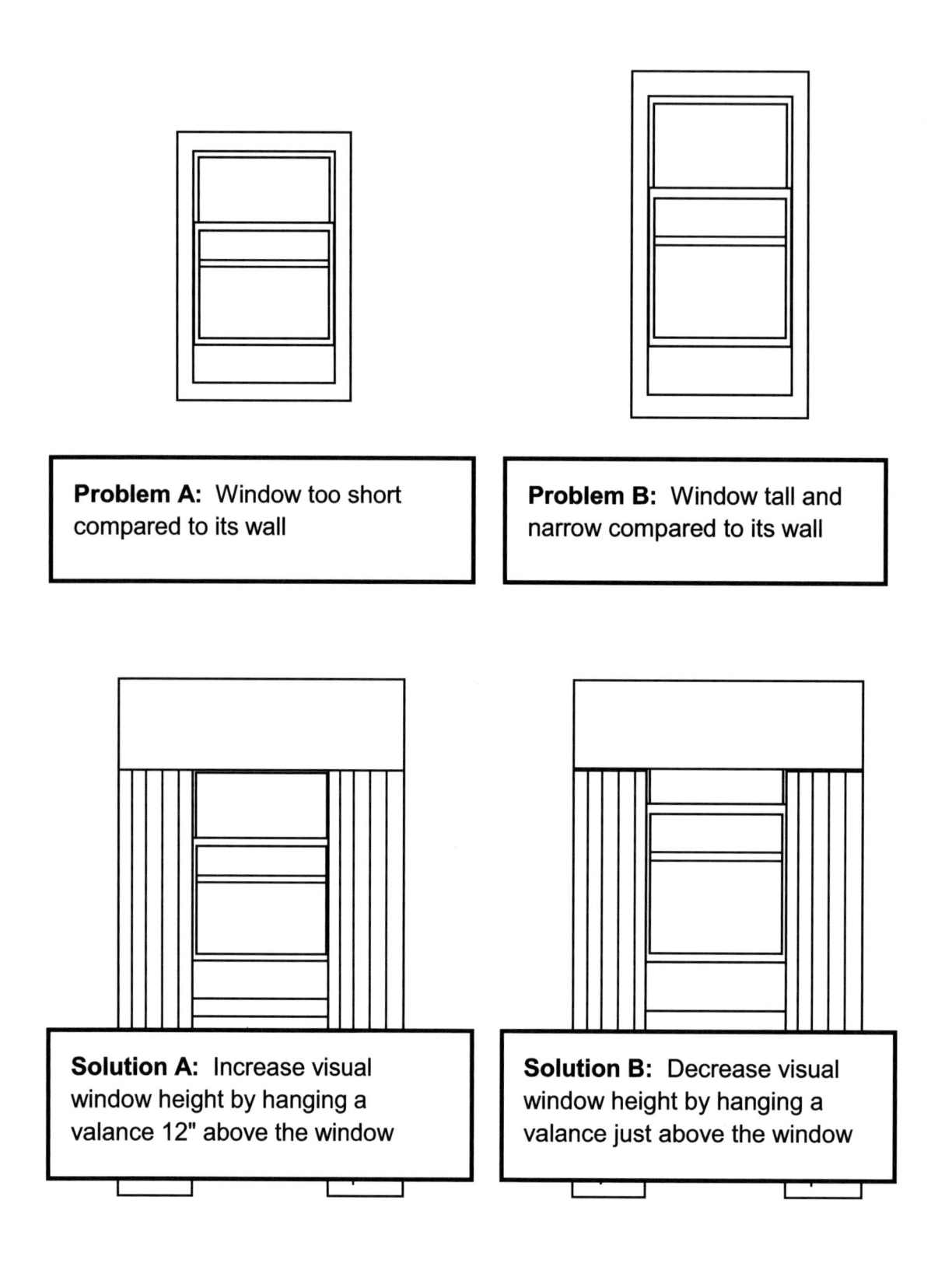

Problem B: Window tall and narrow compared to its wall

Solution A: Increase visual window height by hanging a valance 12" above the window

Solution B: Decrease visual window height by hanging a valance just above the window

DRAPERIES OPTIONS A

Interior Design For Today

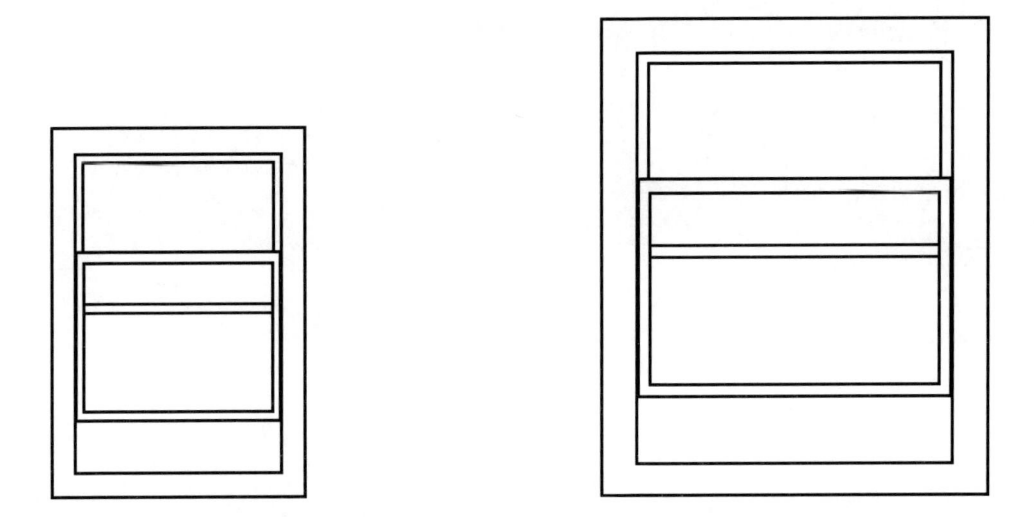

Problem: Windows are different sizes

Solution: a) Hang a single valance across both windows to make appear at the same height b) Hang similar side panels to make appear equal in

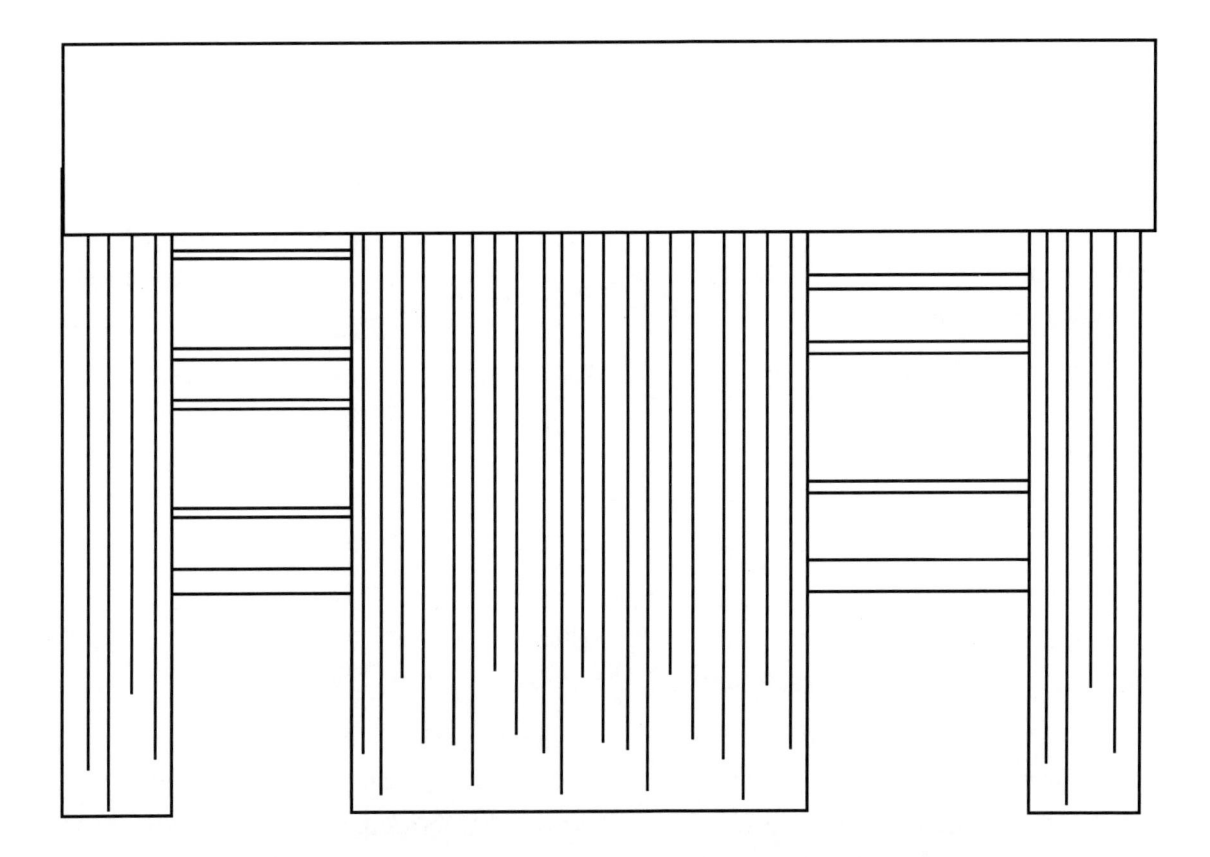

DRAPERIES OPTIONS B

Interior Design For Today

Window Treatment Types

Draperies

Draperies "frame" a window. They are lined curtain panels that are stationary, or can bedrawn open and closed. Draperies are carried to floor-length whenever possible. There are various styles and methods of hanging draperies. The style and method of hanging will depend upon the decorating style of the room.

Pinch-pleated Draperies

Pinch-pleated draperies can be used in a traditional decorating scheme as well as in a modern or contemporary scheme, however the fashion in which they are hung will determine their style.

A traditional room pinch-pleated drapery style will be hung with hooks and eyes onto a traverse rod accompanied with a decorative swag, valance, or cornice. For a more clean-lined modern look, the valance will be omitted and the track will be mounted at ceiling height. For a contemporary room, pinch-pleated draperies might be topped with a simple box-pleated or plain valance.

The header of a pinch-pleated drapery is usually finished with either a Cartridge pleat or a French pleat and the bottom hemmed one-half inch from the floor. Such draperies are opened and closed by pulling on a cord.

An alternative method of hanging pinch-pleated draperies is on a decorative rod. Panels are hooked onto rings that slide across a wooden or metal rod decorated with end caps known as "finials." These rods are mounted roughly six inches above the window, and extend past the window on either side to display the finials to best advantage. They are in full view and their attractive appearance adds charm to any decor.

Unlike traverse rods, decorative rods offer no cord to open and close the draperies. Rods and finials can be chosen from several styles to suit that of a room's style and mood.

Grommet-topped Panels

Another version of window dressing that is hung from a decorative rod is a grommet-topped panel. A lined or unlined fabric panel is fitted with applied grommets equally spaced across the header. The thickness of rod used with these panels is best kept in close proportion to the grommet opening. When opened, these panels fall into symmetrical tidy folds. This look is best used in a contemporary setting.

Tab-top Panels

Tab-top panels are hung full-length from a decorative rod by fabric tabs. This look is casual and fits with a casual contemporary mood. Panels are usually un-lined in a choice of varying fabric weights from heavy to sheer. Refer to your DRAPERIES help.

Rod-pocket Panels

Rod-pocket panels are "shirred" onto an adjustable metal rod through a sewn channel. They are stationary. If fabricated out of a sheer fabric, they are referred to as "sheers" that block out harsh rays of the sun while being see-through. Sheers are generally used along with other window treatments and have a traditional feel to them.

Valance

A valance is used to top a drapery. It is attached to the front and sides of a piece of board mounted horizontally onto the wall above the draperies. The traverse rod is mounted to the under-side of this board and covered by the valance.

The length of the valance is determined by the finished height of the window treatment. To keep the valance in scale, its length will be between one-sixth to one-seventh that of the finished treatment measurement.

Valances may be stiffened with interfacing and lined with the same lining used for the draperies to produce a soft cornice. If the valance is formed with a solid material such as wood, it is referred to as a solid cornice.

Roller & Solar Shades

Roller shades are window treatments that, when pulled down, block out light. Basic, unadorned plasticized shade cloth roller shades are unattractive, however those made of fabric, though not completely opaque, keep out harsh rays of the sun and are more decorative.

Another version of roller shade is referred to as a Solar shade. Solar shades are made from a high-tech mesh material, are not completely opaque, but come in a variety of degrees of opacity and block out UV rays that cause fading in drapery, upholstery, and in carpeting fibers.

Solar shades are best used alone for a clean-lined, sleek, modern look. Fabric roller shades are more conducive to a traditional palette when co-ordinated with draperies.

Roll-up Blinds

Roller blinds (Roll-up blinds) are made of narrow one-half inch slats of bamboo or very thin matchsticks that roll up from the bottom. They have a casual, clean line. Used alone, they fit a contemporary scheme and work well in a casual setting such as a sunroom. Bamboo roll-up blinds work well in a kitchen, as they are easy to wipe clean, and although do not control light completely, they provide enough privacy, while at the same time allow needed light to filter through.

Pull-up Blinds

Pull-up blinds are similar to roll-up blinds in that they are also made with narrow slats of wood or of matchstick bamboo. Because pull-up blinds rise up in folds, they are less bulky than roll-ups and can be used with draperies to give the window treatment a dual purpose, to cut down on daytime's harsh rays of the sun, and when draperies are closed over them, to give complete privacy at night.

Venetian Blinds

Venetian blinds allow light control through slats that are moved up and down to open and close them. Blinds with wide or narrow slats are available in metal, wood, and faux wood in a variety of natural stains and colors. Venetian blinds suit traditional and contemporary spaces. They can be paired with other window treatments or stand alone to provide complete privacy.

Roman Blinds

Roman blinds are made of fabric that folds into pleats as the blind is pulled up. They can be used with any decorating scheme as long as the fabric from which they are made is coherent with the mood of the room. Roman blinds can stand alone or be paired with an additional co-ordinating complimentary treatment. Refer to the HORIZONTAL BLINDS help.

Shoji Screens

Shoji screens are wooden frames with panels of semi-transparent rice paper. They appear as decorative screens, however, they slide side-by-side on tracks to open to, and close off light. Used with sliding glass doors, or full-wall windows, the Shoji screen which is a Japanese influence, fits well into a modern decorating scheme.

Shutters

Wooden shutters are a look suited to any decorating style, alone or combined with other window treatment. For a more modern industrial look, aluminum-finished shutters stand alone.

Choosing Window Treatments

Special Consideration

Window treatments need to be chosen in regard to various window situations. Things to consider when choosing types of window treatment are the size of the room, ceiling height of the room, obstructions needed to work around, window proportions, and positioning, as well as light control and privacy.

Room Size

You have already learned that unity is important to aid coherence in a small room's decor, and that windows should be treated in a way that does not break up coherence.

Window treatments need to be kept simple, either in a solid color or small patterned fabric, so as not to draw attention to them. They will be subtle and blend in, keeping coherency.

Because light colors give the illusion of more space, keeping the window treatments light-colored will contribute toward visually expanding the space as well. If patterned wallpaper is used, use wallcovering in a fabric in the same color as the background color of the wallpaper. If a valance is used, keep it the same color as the draperies.

In a large room, aim for diversity and break up the expanse of walls with treatments in contrasting color to the wall. Use dark colors on the walls and bold patterns on draperies.

If there are two windows on a wall, they can be treated as one to unify the space in a small room. Use a valance that stretches across the top of both windows. Hang an outside drapery panel on each window as well as one centered between the two windows. Sheers or blinds can be added to each window for a layered look. If the room is large, treat each window independently of each other.

Ceiling Height

To visually increase ceiling height, a floor-to-ceiling window treatment can be hung at ceiling height. If a valance is used, keep it at a minimum length and keep the valance in the same fabric as the draperies. Use vertical stripes instead of printed drapery fabric.

To visually lower a high ceiling, break up the space with a horizontal line by adding a valance in a different fabric than the draperies, adding a horizontal blind, and using tie-backs. Hang the window treatment just above the window instead of at ceiling height.

Obstructions

If dressing a window around a heating unit, mount stationary panels on each side of the window and hang an operating blind for privacy or to block out light. Add a valance to complete the look.

Window Size & Proportion

When a window is not in ideal proportion, its visual proportion can be altered by the use of a window treatment. For instance, if the window is proportionately too low, build its height by hanging a valance above the window height so that its bottom just covers the top of the window. Add side drapery panels to complete the look.

If a window is too wide, keep the window treatment inside the outer edges of the window. If the window is too tall and narrow, add a valance to cut the height, extending it and draperies beyond the outside edges of the window. Refer to DRAPERIES OPTIONS A & B.

If two different sized windows are on the same wall, disguise them as above. If the top of one window is higher than the other, use one valance across both windows at the most appropriate height and add drapery panels to the sides and center of the group. If the bottoms of the windows do not line up, add semi-opaque blinds that remain dropped to an equal level below both windows to disguise the difference.

Light Control & Privacy

When deciding on a window treatment, consideration needs to be taken for light control and privacy. Bathroom and bedroom window treatments need to provide complete privacy.

In a bathroom, use of an opaque roller blind or solar shade that can easily be pulled up or down is appropriate. Use it alone or with a valance. An optional treatment is a lined fabric Roman blind.

Use lined draw draperies for the bedroom, or if obstructions prevent this, hang stationary panels together with an opaque blind or shade.

If complete privacy is not an issue, but light control is, a slat-style Venetian blind, semi-opaque solar shade, bamboo pull-up blind, or sheers, alone or together with another treatment, will provide opportunity to let in light while blocking out harmful direct rays of the sun.

Designing with Wall Treatments

Walls cover the greatest expanse of the room. How they are treated will greatly add to the mood and harmony in a room. Although you have already become familiar through this course with color and room color choices for walls, in this lesson, you will study **Types of Paint** and their application to a room, as well as optional wall treatments used to produce mood and their ability to harmonize with the style of the room. These include **Wallpaper, Paneling**, **Decorative Mouldings,** and the addition of **Natural Materials** such as stone, brick, and wood.

Paint & Its Application

Paint Choices

Painting walls is the easiest and least-expensive way to up-date a color palette and affect mood in a room, and is a favored choice of wall treatment of many, but all paint is not alike. Choice between oil-based and water-based paint needs to be decided upon as well as sheen

Latex Paint

Water-based paint is known as latex. **Latex Paint** is easy to use and clean up is with soap and water. Latex paint comes in a variety of finishes that need to be considered before planning their application.

The appropriateness of a paint finish is determined by its scrubability and sheen. *Flat* latex is a dull finish known as matte. A matte finish absorbs light and appears stagnant. It shows fingerprints, stains, and is not easily cleaned. Even so, flat latex paint has the advantage of hiding imperfections, and is best used in a situation where uneven wall surfaces are a concern.

A low-sheen finish provides a desired affect when the mood is subtle and will be used on living room, dining room, and bedroom walls where cleanability is less of an issue. A step up from a matte finish in the way of sheen is a *low-luster* finish known by various manufacturers as "eggshell," "suede," or "velvet." This semi-matte finish has a low sheen, but not as dull a finish as flat paint. It is scrubable and easier to clean, and is the choice most often made for most walls.

A next step up from low-luster is a "Silk" or "Satin" finish with a little more sheen. It is used in children's rooms, kitchens, bathrooms, and hallways where the advantage of scrubability is important.

Gloss paint comes in two different sheens, "semi-gloss" and "high-gloss." Gloss, as its name implies, has a glossy finish. Gloss paint provides a hard, durable surface that cleans most easily, and therefore is the right choice for door and window trims, baseboards, and mouldings. Gloss paint's durability makes it a practical choice for wall surfaces where moisture may be a problem, such as in a bathroom or laundry room.

Unless a slick, high-tech look is what you are going for, when the choice needs to be made between semi-gloss or high-gloss, semi-gloss is preferred for walls, whereas wood-work can handle either depending upon the individual preference and mood of the room. A semi-gloss finish will stand out less than a high-gloss, and suits a more relaxed, subtle mood. A high-gloss finish exudes a more traditional, formal look.

A qualified painter will know to apply a prime coat prior to the first coat of paint. Because latex paint is quick drying, a second coat can be applied within 6 hours. Before a second coat is applied, the color can be adjusted if the first coat appears too light, too dark, too intense, or too muted. However, do not decide if the color needs to be corrected until the painted wall is completely dry, as paint usually appears darker when wet.

To darken the color, black can be added. To lighten it, white can be added. To tone down a color that is too intense, brown or "burnt umber" can be added. To deepen or intensify a color, minute amounts of "raw umber" or "raw sienna" pigment can be added.

Alkyd Paint

Latex paints today are much improved in durability since years ago when oil-based paint was the paint of choice. However, oil-based paints have also improved in that harmful fumes and lead content have been eliminated.

Oil-base paints with no lead content are known as "alkyd," and are still a preference where a hard durable surface is of essence. Alkyd paint is available in either a satin, semi-gloss, or high-gloss finish, and interior use is usually restricted to wet areas or to doors, window trim, baseboards, and mouldings.

The drying time of oil-based alkyd paint is 24 hours, and it is imperative that the paint is completely dry before putting on the next coat. Because alkyd paint is thinner than latex, it requires more coats to finish. Painting with alkyd is labor-intensive and time-consuming, and therefore, more expensive than painting with latex.

Applying Paint Color

Since you have already studied color in Unit II, a study on paint color here will highlight some of what you have already learned, but also help to put this knowledge into perspective regarding the actual application of painted color.

Color and Effect

Red is a very exciting and dramatic color. It is believed to stimulate appetite, and is a good choice for a dining room if bold color is in the plan.

Yellow is a bright color that emits a sense of cheer. It gives a room a warm, sunny look and is inviting used in a kitchen, dinette, or laundry room.

Orange is bright and cheery and adds flare to a contemporary space. Used in its pure state on one wall in a dining room or children's bedroom, creates an accent wall as the focal point in the room.

Blue has a calm, clean effect and brings relaxation to any room in the house.

Green links with nature and brings the outdoors inside. It is restful and easy to live with, and is valued as a basic in interior design.

Violet is soothing and glamorous, and brings these characteristics with it when used on bedroom walls.

White gives a sense of purity. It is widely used in interiors, especially on ceilings, doors, baseboards, mouldings, and trims, to give a clean, crisp look and feel to a room.

Paint Color Tricks

Because color looks different on a wall than it does on a paint chip, test patches of two or three similar hues in different intensities should be painted before deciding on the exact paint color. These, painted against a white primed background, will show forth the true color.

Because paint color is affected by natural or artificial lighting, test colors should be viewed in the room at different times of the day to help determine which hue is most appropriate. Paint on the expanse of a wall looks more intense than on a smaller surface, and can be overwhelming, therefore, choose the test color that is least bold.

The brightness of the room can be established by the wall color. Light colors make a space appear brighter and larger and are more appropriate for dimly or poorly lit rooms, while dark colors, on the other hand, make a room appear smaller, and are more suitable for well-lit, large spaces.

A trick applied to make a low ceiling appear higher, is to paint the ceiling white. To make a high ceiling appear lower, paint it a dark color.

When matching wall paint color to a fabric color, choose a shade lighter or darker than the fabric, as there is no perfect match, and if there is not enough of a difference between the colors, the affect will be unpleasant.

Painting Techniques

There are various paint techniques that can be applied to walls for special effects. We will touch on only a few.

The application of a brushed-on, textured line, is the technique referred to as *"strie."* A glaze is applied over a dry base coat of paint and a "dragging brush" is "dragged" downward on the wet glaze to produce vertical lines.

Walls can also be *"sponged"* to produce a textured look. Glaze is sponged onto a flat base coat. The variation between the flat paint and glossy glaze gives the impression of texture. The glaze may be tinted with color before being sponged onto the wall to produce a multi-colored effect.

Optional Wall Treatments

Wallpaper

Wallpapers are available in a variety of textures, colors, and designs, as well as types. Embossed wallpaper has a raised textured pattern. Flocked wallpaper has a raised fabric design that feels velvety to the touch. Both embossed and flocked wallpapers are opulent in style. Grasscloth wallpapers are embedded with strips of grass that have been glued onto the paper to give it a natural look and feel. Its textured surface adds warmth to a contemporary setting.

Most wallpapers are vinyl coated for cleanability, durability, and stain-resistance, and are "strippable." Vinyl-coated wallpaper has a paper base. Its surface is spray-coated with acrylic-vinyl or polyvinyl chloride (PVC) making the surface scrubable.

Coated *fabric wallpaper* has a fabric base that is coated with liquid vinyl or acrylic. The design is printed on the vinyl coating. Such wallpaper is referred to as "breathable" and is used in rooms where moisture is not a problem, such as living rooms and bedrooms.

Paper-backed solid vinyl wallpaper has a solid surface with a "pulp" paper backing. This solid surface is very scrubable and peels off easily when stripped. It is stain and grease resistant, as well as moisture-resistant, and therefore appropriate for use in high-moisture areas such as bathrooms.

Fabric-backed vinyl wallpaper has a solid vinyl surface laminated to a fabric backing and is most durable.

Paper wallpaper has a decorative print layer of paper on a paper backing and does not have a vinyl coating. It is not durable and scrubable, however, has a beauty all to its own.

Wallpapers are available in single and double rolls in differing widths. In general, the number of square feet covered per single roll is 30, and 60 per double roll. When ordering wallpaper, calculate the number of square footage to be covered by measuring the area of the wall, its height x its width, making no allowance for doors and windows, as these will have to be cut out of full sheets. Make allowance for pattern repeat waste. Once you know the total square footage to be covered, divide that number by 30 to determine how many rolls of wallpaper are needed.

Hanging wallpaper is the job of a professional. A paperhanger will need to know if the wallpaper you have selected has been purchased in single or double rolls, as well as the length of the pattern repeat. He will examine the walls and prepare them for installation.

If the wall has existing wallpaper, it will need to be removed. If the walls are new sheetrock, they will need to be painted with a coat of primer and let dry before wallpaper can be applied.

Natural Wall Materials

Natural materials such as stone and brick add warmth to an interior. Stone, slate, and brick are most often used as a wall material around a fireplace. Completely covering one wall in a room with stone veneer or brick provides a stunning accent wall. This treatment is best applied to a large open space such as that of a family room, or a large, open-concept living room. The look and feel of these natural materials used in this fashion has a modernistic edge to it.

Wood Paneling and Moulding

Solid wood paneled walls are appropriate in a traditional setting for an office, den, or dining room, however, very costly. A most cost effective approach to obtaining a similar formal traditional look is to use wood mouldings. Refer to theARCHITECTURAL DETAIL help and handout to see how decorative ceiling moulding, crown moulding, picture moulding, chair rail, wainscoting, and baseboard can be applied at a fraction of the cost.

For a more refined modern look, walls can be paneled with "flitches," 4 X 8-foot panels of ¾ - inch veneered plywood. These flitches are installed side-by-side across the whole width of the wall with a ½ - inch space, called a "reveal," between panels.

Designing with Flooring

There are various floor coverings that can be applied for beauty and practicality, including solid surface flooring such as hardwood, wood laminate, ceramic and stone tile, and vinyl. An optional choice in flooring is wall-to-wall carpeting. In this lesson we will discuss the options, their advantages, and their use.

Solid Surface Floor Covering

Wood Flooring

Hardwood is a durable floor covering that adds beauty to any decor. There are various grades of hardwood to choose from as well as stains and colors on wood grains. Choosing the color of stain and type of hardwood are dependent on the mood of the design scheme. Dark stains add elegance and formality. They suit either traditional or modern interiors. Light stains or bleached wood are suitable for casual, contemporary spaces.

When choosing a hardwood for your room, study sample boards in the room and under different lighting conditions to determine which color is a preference.

Hardwood is protected with a sealer and at least two coats of polyurethane. Strip hardwood comes in 1 - 3 inch wide tongue and groove strips that are invisibly nailed to a subfloor. Plank flooring comes in 3 - 6 inch wide boards that are nailed or screwed to a subfloor and holes are covered with plugs. Parquet flooring comes in small strips that form squares that are laid in alternating directions to form a geometric pattern.

Engineered wood is a flooring material made from layers of wood glued together and looks and functions as solid wood flooring but is less expensive.

Wood laminate flooring is a wood product made to resemble hardwood. It has a plywood base with a layer of wood veneer.

Wood is a rich looking, long-lasting flooring that can be refinished many times over during the lifetime of a home. Although wood flooring is an expensive flooring choice, it is a good investment and preferred for main living areas such as living rooms and dining rooms.

Laminate Flooring

Laminate flooring is not to be confused with wood laminate. Laminate flooring is made with a wood-composition core over which a resin-based surface is applied. The surface material contains a photographic image of either wood, stone, or marble so that, when installed, the product resembles the real thing.

Laminate comes in 4-foot long 3/8-inch boards with a snap-together tongue-and-groove system that does not require nailing so that the floor "floats." Though laminate may imitate wood flooring, its extremely hard surface is less comfortable to walk on. Laminate is used in a very low-budget job for living room, dining room, kitchen, and bedroom applications. It cannot be used if there is an issue with excessive moisture.

Ceramic & Stone Tile

Ceramic and stone tile provide a durable solid-surface material that comes in a variety of colors and patterns in squares of up to 13-inches wide.

Tile is laid in various ways to form symmetrical or asymmetrical patterns and different colors may be inter-mixed to add even more interest.

Although most ceramic tile is glazed, quarry tile and slate are unglazed and will need to be treated once installed.

Ceramic and stone tile is used in high-traffic areas for durability, as well in areas where moisture is an issue, such as laundry rooms, kitchens, bathrooms, as well as entrance ways.

Vinyl

Vinyl flooring is resilient and has a cushiony effect making it a "quieter" flooring surface than either hardwood, wood laminate, ceramic tile, or stone, and is more comfortable underfoot. Vinyl is available in a variety of colors and patterns and is laid in 6 or 12-foot widths or in square tiles and is glued to the sub-floor.

hardwood
& wood

FLOORING SAMPLES A

© Copyright 2013

ceramic tile

stone tile

& vinyl

FLOORING SAMPLES B

© Copyright 2013

Carpeting

Carpet Choices

Carpet is the floor covering of choice if quiet, comfort, and warmth underfoot is what is desired, as it is a natural insulator that absorbs sound.

Carpeting comes in various textures, colors, patterns, sculptural effects, fibers, and piles. Its cost is based on fiber, construction, and quality. Wall-to-wall installation includes carpet padding and the best padding afforded is the best choice.

Wool Carpeting

A good quality carpet is durable and soil-resistant. Wool carpeting is the best quality because its texture is soft and springy. However, wool on its own is not durable, nor is it mildew-resistant, therefore, it is usually mixed with synthetic fibers to increase its durability and resistance to mold and mildew. Wool carpeting is the most expensive carpeting available and only used on high-budget interiors.

Synthetic Carpeting

Synthetic fibers, including nylon, acrylics, polyesters, and polypropylenes, are combined together to produce the most wool-like look and softness, while being durable, mothproof, and mold and mildew-resistent. Most carpeting is treated for stain-resistance with a "Scotchguard," or "Teflon," treatment, however, it is important to confirm this when purchasing carpeting, otherwise it will have to be treated after installation.

Carpet Texture

The durability of carpeting depends on its type of fiber, but also on the density of its pile "tufts," as well as on the "twist" in the yarn and its weight. The longer and denser the pile, the heavier the weight, and the better quality and more expensive the carpet.

Varieties of textures and patterns are created by the cut of loops of yarn referred to as "pile." "Plush" velvety smooth carpeting has a dense long-level cut loop and a twist to the strands of yarn producing a very deep, rich, soft, "deep-pile" carpeting. Its surface takes on a different appearance when vacuumed. Its pile is pushed at different angles that take light differently causing a desired "shading" effect. Plush carpet is the most luxurious, "shades" the most, and is the most expensive. It is used in formal settings for living rooms and bedrooms.

"Saxony" textured pile has smooth level-cut loops that are shorter than plush carpeting, and therefore less expensive. Because of Saxony's twisted strands, its appearance is as plush, however, its less-deep pile is not as soft underfoot. Densities of Saxony vary and need to be considered when deciding upon quality. This style is less formal than a plush textured carpet and is used widely throughout living rooms and bedrooms on a moderate-budget.

When yarns have a strong twist to form a curly texture, the pile is referred to as "frieze," or if lengths of yarn are very long, it is considered a "shag." Shag carpet may have either level loops or cut loops. Its look has a trendy, contemporary edge that fits well with a more modern decorating scheme. Frieze carpeting or shag rugs are used for either a casual or formal look in a living room or bedroom on a moderate budget.

Carpeting that has a combination of both cut and un-cut loops, forming sculptured effects, is considered a Cut-and-Loop pile and is less formal-looking than cut pile. Other variations of sculpted carpeting includes a combination of high and low loops, or low and high-cut loops.

A more casual-look carpeting, textured with un-cut large and knobby looped pile, is referred to as "Berber." Level-loop Berber is tightly woven, very durable, resists dirt, and can be easily cleaned. It is appropriate for high-traffic areas. When a multi-level loop texture is formed with two or three different heights of loops, a patterned effect is created.

A least-formal style of carpeting is made from straw-like natural fibers such as hemp, sisal, and jute, and is used in a very casual space such as a sun room or porch. However, when bound with a wide contrasting trim, also works well in a living room or dining room with an informal contemporary design.

'Add Carpet For Warmth'

Gathe

© Copyright 2013

ring Carpet Samples

Interior Design For Today

UNIT II DESIGN PROJECT Part B

1. Complete a **LIGHTING STYLE Worksheet** for each of your Living Room, Bedroom, and Dining Room, as well as for Stafford's Living/Dining Room. Refer to the LIVING ROOM FURNITURE STYLE Worksheet for help. Label your LIGHTING STYLE Worksheets in a similar manner. Either draw pictures of lighting and lamps for your rooms based on your Lighting Layouts, or collect them from magazines and apply them to each of your LIGHTING STYLE Worksheets. Decide on style, keeping it coherent with the style and mood you have decided upon for your room.

2. Complete a **WINDOW TREATMENT Worksheet** for each of your Living Room, Bedroom, and Dining Room, as well as for Stafford's Living/Dining Room. Refer to the SAMPLE WINDOW TREATMENT Worksheet for help. Set up your WINDOW TREATMENT Worksheets in a similar manner.

Either draw pictures of the drapery style and mounting hardware you intend to use in your design, or collect them from magazines Apply them to each of your WINDOW TREATMENT Worksheets. Keep style coherent with the style and mood you have decided upon for your room.

3. Complete a **BED TREATMENT Worksheet** for your Bedroom. Refer to the SAMPLE BED TREATMENT Worksheet for help. Set up your BED TREATMENT Worksheet in a similar manner. Either draw pictures of the bed and bedding, or collect them from magazines and apply them to your BED TREATMENT Worksheet. Label each piece of bedding.

Name: _____

Room: _____

LIGHTING STYLE Worksheet

Name: Peter Forest

Room: Master Bedroom

Date: Sept. 4, 2xxx

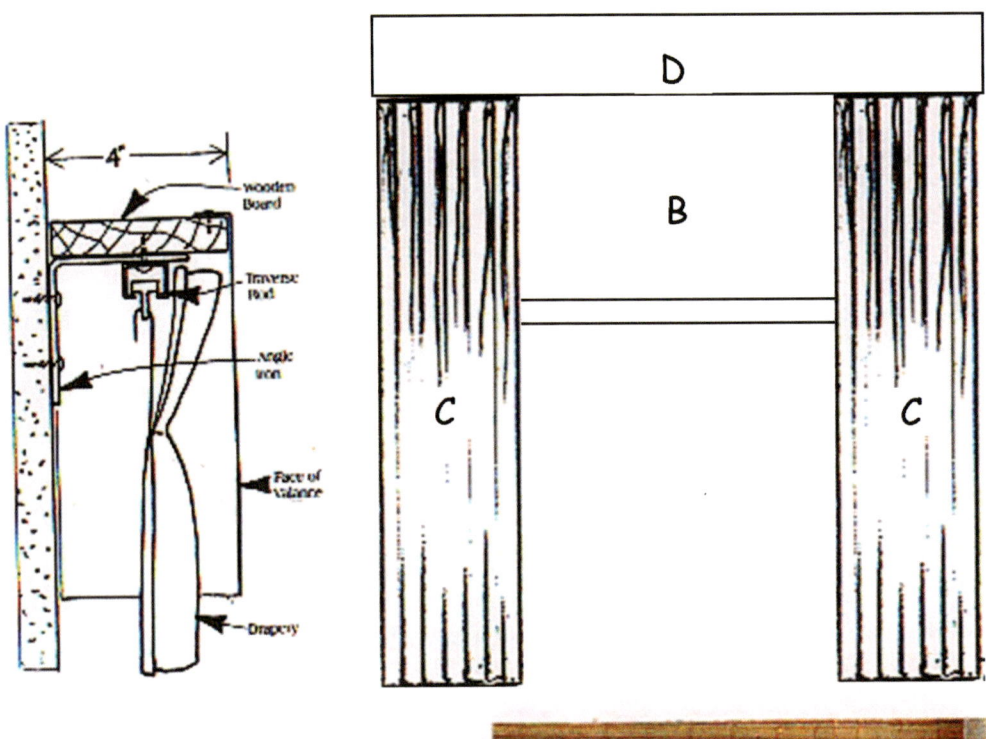

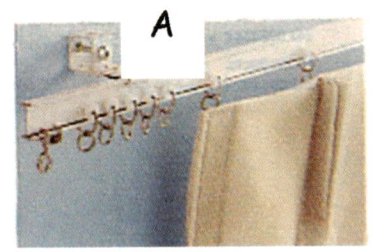

A. DRAPERY HARDWARE
B. ROLL UP BLIND
C. DRAPERY PANELS
D. VALANCE

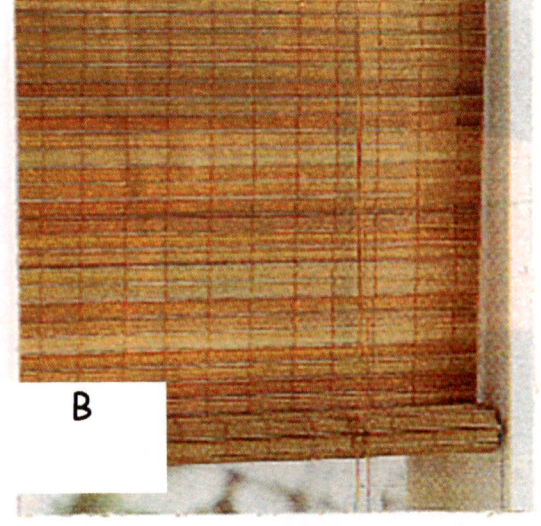

SAMPLE WINDOW TREATMENT Worksheet

Name: Peter Forest

Room: Master Bedroom

Date: Dec. 23, 2XXX

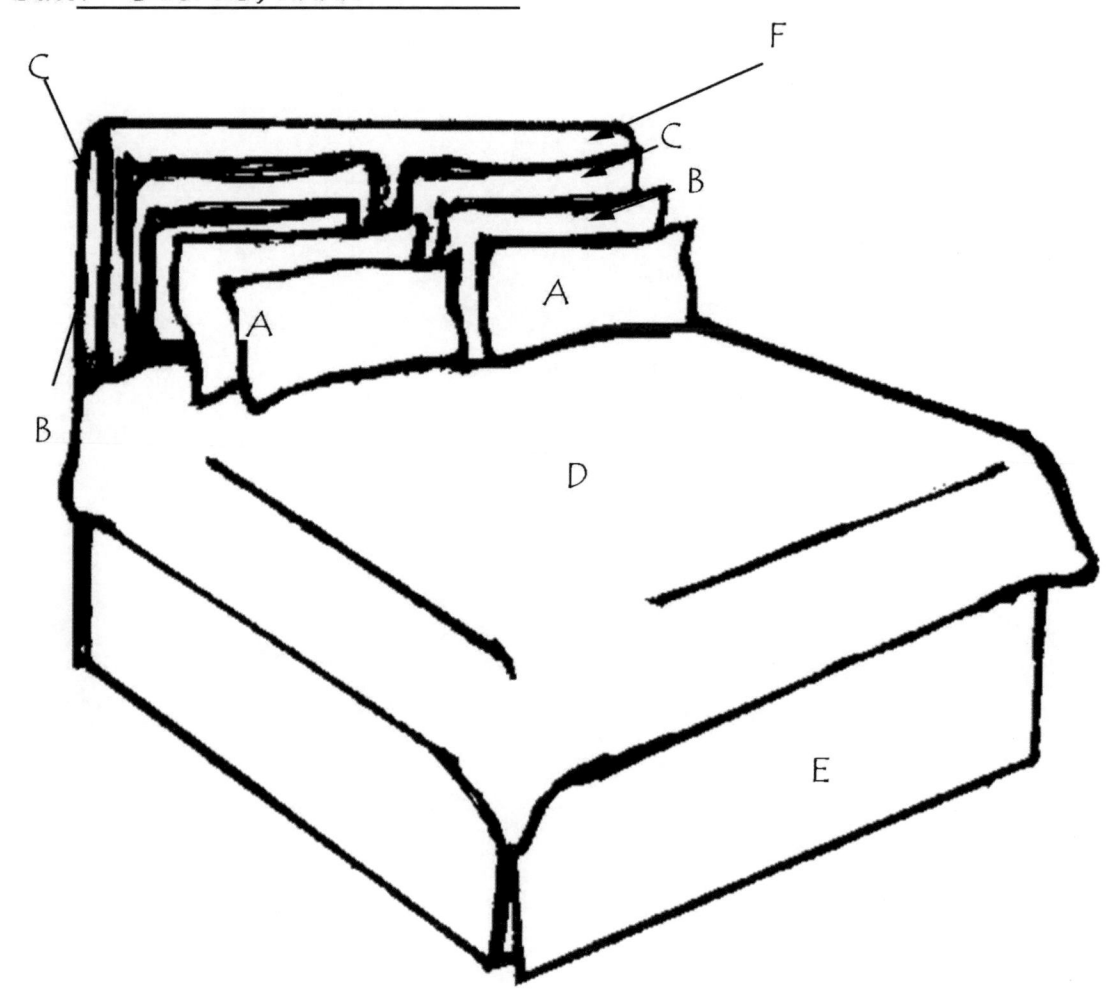

A Pillows
B Pillows
C Pillows
D Duvet Cover
E Bedskirt
F Padded Headboard

SAMPLE BED TREATMENT Worksheet

Interior Design
For Today

4. Complete a **ROOM WORKSHEET Part B** for each of your Living Room, Bedroom, and Dining Room, as well as for Stafford's Living/Dining Room. Make copies of the ROOM WORKSHEET Part B. Answer the questions in detail.

ROOM WORKSHEET

Name: _____ *Date:* _____

Client: _____ *Room:* _____

Furniture

- List each major piece of furniture you intend to use and give a detailed description of it. Identify each piece with a corresponding letter on your Furniture Layout.

A _____
B _____
C _____
D _____
E _____
F _____
G _____

Lighting

- List each major lighting fixture and lamp you intend to use. Identify each piece with corresponding number on your LIGHT STYLE Worksheet.

1. _____
2. _____
3. _____
4. _____
5. _____
6. _____
7. _____

Interior Design For Today

Pg. 2

Flooring

- Describe the flooring treatment you are implementing into your design.

Wall Treatment

- Describe the wall treatment you are implementing into your design. Refer to your Color Scheme Board. Give detail of paint choices, including reason for your choice. Include a similar description of how you will handle mouldings and trim.

Window Treatments

- Describe the window treatments you are intending to implement for each window in the room, including color and fabric choices, drapery hardware choices, method of hanging, and the reason for your choices. Refer to your WINDOW TREATMENT Worksheet and Color Scheme Board. Identify each different type of window with a symbol on a copy of your floorplan to be attached to this schedule.

Interior Design For Today

Upholstery

- Describe the upholstery treatment of soft furnishings you are implementing into your design, including color and fabric choices and reason for the choices. Refer to your Color Scheme Board.

_____
_____
_____
_____

Bed Treatment

- Describe the Bed Treatment you are implementing into your design, including color and fabric choices and reason for the choices. Refer to your BED TREATMENT Worksheet and Color Scheme Board.

_____
_____
_____
_____
_____

Summary

- Define your general design objective in this room and how you have attempted to achieve it. Consider architectural detailing, function, style, mood, and harmony, as well as detail of finishing touches.

_____
_____
_____
_____
_____
_____
_____

Kitchens & Bathrooms

Interior design is not limited to the living room, dining room, and bedroom. **Kitchens and Bathrooms** are also spaces that will need your services as an interior designer. Undergoing kitchen and bathroom projects mainly fall into the hands of renovators who will employ the services of trades people such as a plumber and electrician to complete the task of providing updates that are up to code standard. As an interior designer, your job is to design the space and oversee the project from beginning to completion, therefore it is important that you are familiar with all aspects of kitchen and bathroom design.

In this lesson we will give an overview of the responsibility of an interior designer in the design of a kitchen and bathroom. You will need, however, to do your homework when working on such a project to familiarize yourself with kitchen and bathroom fixtures and appliances available in your area.

Designing a Kitchen

Design Strategy

The first step in designing a kitchen is to fill out a questionnaire that helps to identify how much change will take place to accommodate your client's preferences in a kitchen remodel. Trace a copy of the KITCHEN DESIGN QUESTIONNAIRE provided. Fill in pertinent information regarding structural changes, style, color preferences, detail regarding preferences in cabinetry, surfacing materials, flooring, etc. Familiarize yourself with the kind of questions you will need to ask your client prior to taking on a design project for this room. As an interior designer, you will be able to discuss the remodeling needs and preferences of your client and offer suggestions. You will analyze the kitchen and adjoining areas, decide on potential structural changes, and create working drawings for each of your trades.

Recognize that, depending on the scope of the job, your expertise as an interior designer will be challenged in the area of kitchen design, and therefore it is imperative that you visit kitchen showrooms to familiarize yourself with what is available. You will need to link and work closely with an electrician, plumber, and if a complete renovation will be taking place, with a contractor. Your responsibility will be to oversee the project from start to finish.

Determining Kitchen Needs

The Kitchen is the hub of activity in the home and although needs to be practical, functional, and efficient, it is territory for good design in that it takes on a certain mood and style just as does other rooms of a home. When interviewing a client regarding his/her needs and wants in a kitchen, you will want to make a list of these, and as budget permits, add them into the design. You can expect that your client has already prepared her own portfolio of magazine pictures, brochures, and notes, and therefore, with her considerations and your design expertise, you will be able to present a design that incorporates the style and functional qualities on the wish list.

KITCHEN DESIGN QUESTIONNAIRE

CLIENT: _____

HOME ADDRESS: _____

JOB LOCATION: _____

DATE:

PHONE:

- What is the main function of your kitchen? What are secondary functions?

_____

_____

- How many cooks share the kitchen? How often?

_____

_____

- What is the cooking style, simple, or elaborate meals? Is a lot of baking involved?

_____

_____

- How many people are cooked for on a regular basis? How many on special occassions?

_____

_____

- What applianced do you use most? Are they sufficient, or do you envision additional appliances to be a help? If so, what are they?

_____

_____

- Do you have sufficient workspace around major appliances, sinks, as well as for secondary activities?

_____

_____

Interior Design For Today

- Describe your storage situation. Is it adequate and efficient for equipment, canned goods, dishware, etc? If not, is there an adjacent closet or small room that can be incorporated into the floorplan?

___

- Describe your kitchen arrangement. Is a work triangle in place and is there easy access from one work station to the next?

___

- Describe your lighting and power situattion. Is lighting where you need it? Do you have access to power outlets where they are needed?

___

- Describe the architectural qualities of your kitchen. How high is the ceiling? Is the size of the space small, or large? Do windows let in a lot of natural light, or is the kitchen dark?

___

- How do you feel about your kitchen? Do you like the "look" of it, or do you want a completely new look and feel? Do you prefer an uncluttered look, or one that is more "personalized." Describe your choice.

___

Interior Design For Today

In order to get an accurate feel for needs of the space, your KITCHEN DESIGN QUESTIONNAIRE will help you to pinpoint exactly how the space will be used.

Architectural features of the room need to be noted including ceiling height and square footage, as well as natural lighting. On occasion, a client will want square footage added to the room, removing walls to open the kitchen up to other rooms, or the addition of windows.

Storage needs will have to be addressed as well as preparation surfaces. If the kitchen is open to other rooms in the home, the spaces will need to be unified by keeping the scheme coherent from one room to the other. If a message center, or computer desk is a need, it will have to be fitted into the square footage of the space in a way that is unobtrusive to the flow of traffic and work areas.

Design Options

The basics to a kitchen are a stove, sink, refrigerator, food preparation and cleanup areas, as well as storage. Once these are in place, other aspects of kitchen design can be considered.

The kitchen is one room in the house where a variety of natural materials are mixed to achieve hard-wearing surfaces in wood, stainless steel, copper, granite, and stone. Wood is warm and counterbalances the cool sleekness of juxtaposed stainless steel and gives a kitchen a clean state-of-the-art edge to kitchen design.

Kitchen cabinets are available in a variety of woods and styles. In a sleek, modern kitchen, flush un-decorative surfaces dictate the style, while a more traditional kitchen will include decorative furniture-like cabinets and the room will be adorned with mouldings and pilasters.

A large kitchen provides the most opportunity for creative decor, but needs a design that incorporates efficiency. A center island is a popular choice. A cooktop or sink can be built into it, or it can be used for food preparation, serving, and if an extension is added to the countertop, or a raised bar, seating can be gathered around it.

When considering layout, a few options exist. One is the "unfitted" kitchen featuring freestanding, furniture-like cabinetry. Another is the "fitted" or built-in kitchen where cabinets are attached around the room side by side with no breaks for a stream-lined look. The fitted kitchen provides maximum storage and counter space with standard built-in cabinetry. Variety is brought into a fitted kitchen by altering upper cabinet heights, extending upper cabinet units to the counter, by using decorative glass or metals on upper cabinets, as well as by incorporating open shelving into the design.

An open-concept kitchen gives opportunity for a dinette or breakfast eating area. You will want to take advantage of the opportunity to incorporate extra window openings around this section, or sliding glass or French doors to allow in a maximum amount of welcomed natural light. If the space is small, instead of a table and free standing chairs, a built-in banquette will suffice.

The Work Triangle

An efficient kitchen is broken into work zones and uses a "work triangle" to incorporate the main work centers of the sink, stove or cooktop, and the refrigerator. When drawing up a floorplan, the work triangle will be an effective tool in placement of these work stations. Each side of the triangle should measure at least four feet but no more than nine feet.

Work zones for preparing food, cooking, and cleaning up, will be designed around the work station triangle as well. For instance, a section of counter top near the refrigerator will be used for unloading groceries, a stretch of counter top at least one foot wide is needed on either side of the cooktop for utensils and preparation. Surface space for a cutting board for vegetable preparation is needed near the sink as well as space on one side of the sink for a drainboard. Although the dishwasher is not considered part of the work triangle, it it best installed beside the sink for easy access. The microwave needs to be positioned where countertop is available to set down a hot dish.

Other work zones are arranged outside the work triangle and located where most efficient. For instance, a coffee maker and toaster will be placed in close proximity to the eating area and out of the way of the work triangle so as not to interfere with work traffic.

Refer to WORK TRIANGLE A and B. There are a variety of ways to incorporate the work triangle into the kitchen. In the planning stage, assess your space to design its use efficiently.

Another aspect to consider when designing floor space of a kitchen is the space used for traffic. A minimum of four feet is required between counter sections for a free flow of traffic, the opening of refrigerator, oven, and dishwasher doors and pull out drawers. To keep walking distance at a minimum between work stations, keep the refrigerator and other doors swinging open away from the work triangle.

Balance And Harmony In Design

In kitchen design, as in the design of any other room, the rules of balance and harmony need to be applied to the space. Once the work triangle is established as well as its accompanying work zones, the arrangement of cabinetry can be addressed.

To obtain a clean, un-broken, harmonious design, cabinetry needs to be arranged in a fashion where visual weight is balanced out. Refer to KITCHEN BALANCE A, B, and C. Observe **Fig. 1** and compare it with **Fig. 2**. Which design appears more balanced? Compare **Fig. 3** and **Fig. 4**. Cabinet height should follow the height of the window for best balance. Another factor should be observed when compiling cabinetry. Upper units should line up with lower units. Compare **Fig. 5** and **Fig. 6**. Not only should cabinet doors line up, but so also should hardware. Compare **Fig. 7** and **Fig. 8**. Consider **Fig. 9** and **Fig. 10**. What keeps **Fig. 10** in better balance than **Fig. 9**? Place tall, visually heavy elements at the far ends of the kitchen.

Another element of design to consider when observing cabinet balance, is the space between the top of upper cabinetry and the ceiling. If the space is more than a foot, it can be left open, however, if it is less than a foot, it will appear out of balance. To adjust this imperfection, cabinetry should either be extended to the ceiling, or a bulkhead framed in to fill in this space.

Counter Space

An ideal kitchen makes the most of counter space. It keeps an uninterrupted flow with tall appliances or cabinets at either end of a bank of cabinetry. Refer to COUNTER SPACE & LIGHTING for help. Study the drawings to get an understanding of the best way to gain counter space, including the use of the island or peninsula.

Kitchen Cabinetry

Choosing a cabinet style follows the same procedure as choosing furniture for other rooms. If you want to create a contemporary mood, choose cabinetry with clean, sleek, straight lines. If you want to create a traditional mood, use cabinetry with traditional style detailing.

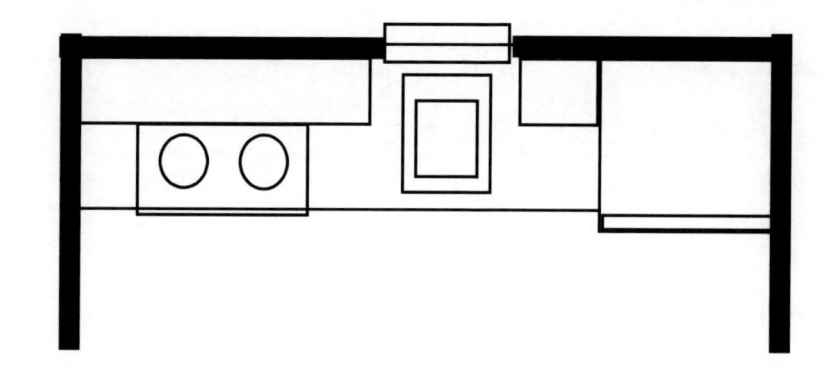

Single-wall Kitchen

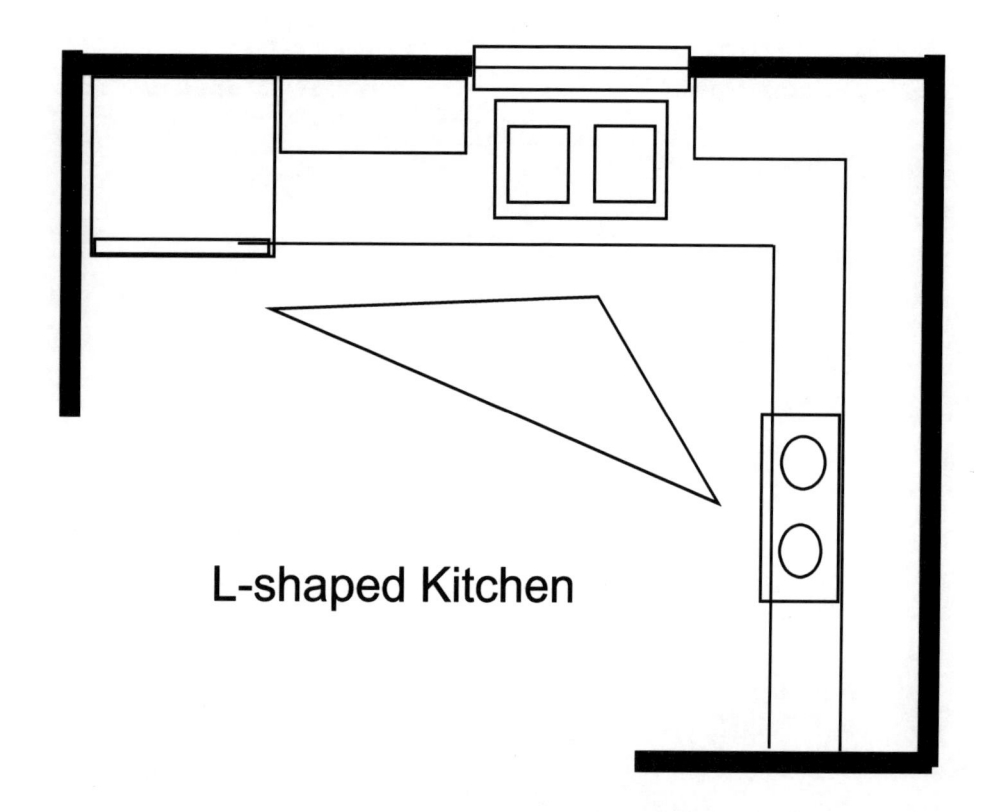

L-shaped Kitchen

WORK TRIANGLE A

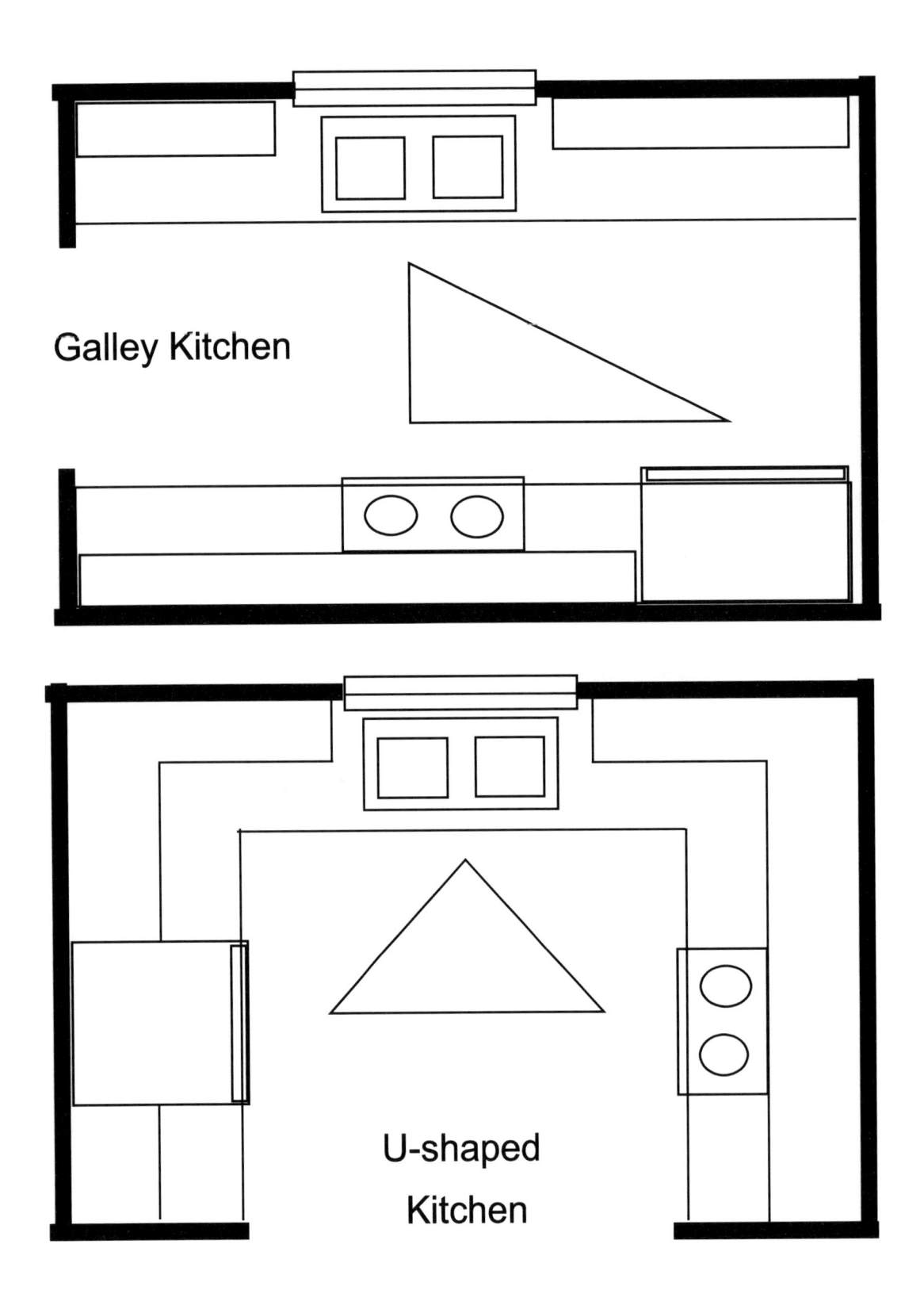

Galley Kitchen

U-shaped Kitchen

WORK TRIANGLE A

Interior Design
For Today

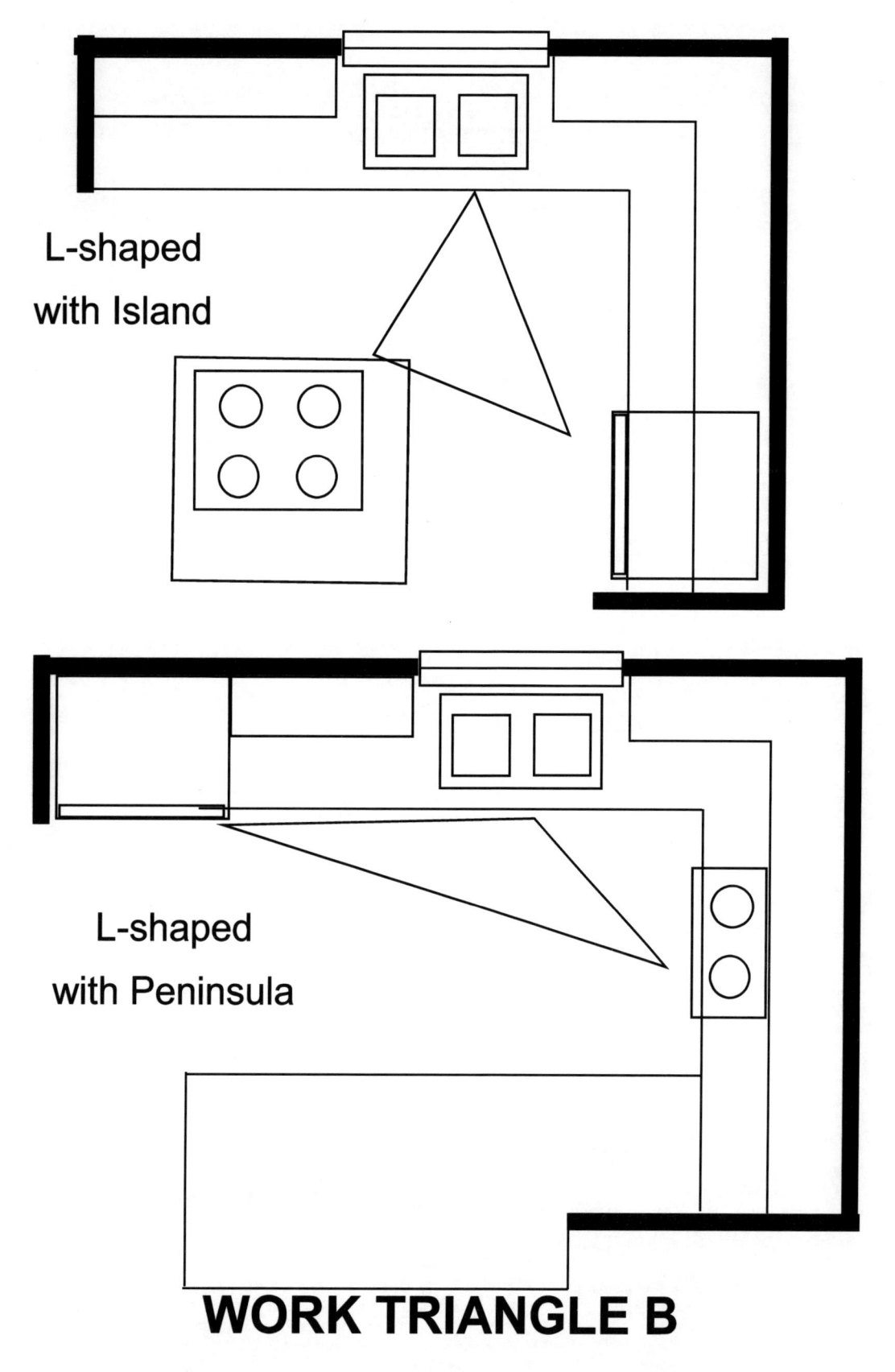

L-shaped
with Island

L-shaped
with Peninsula

WORK TRIANGLE B

Interior Design For Today

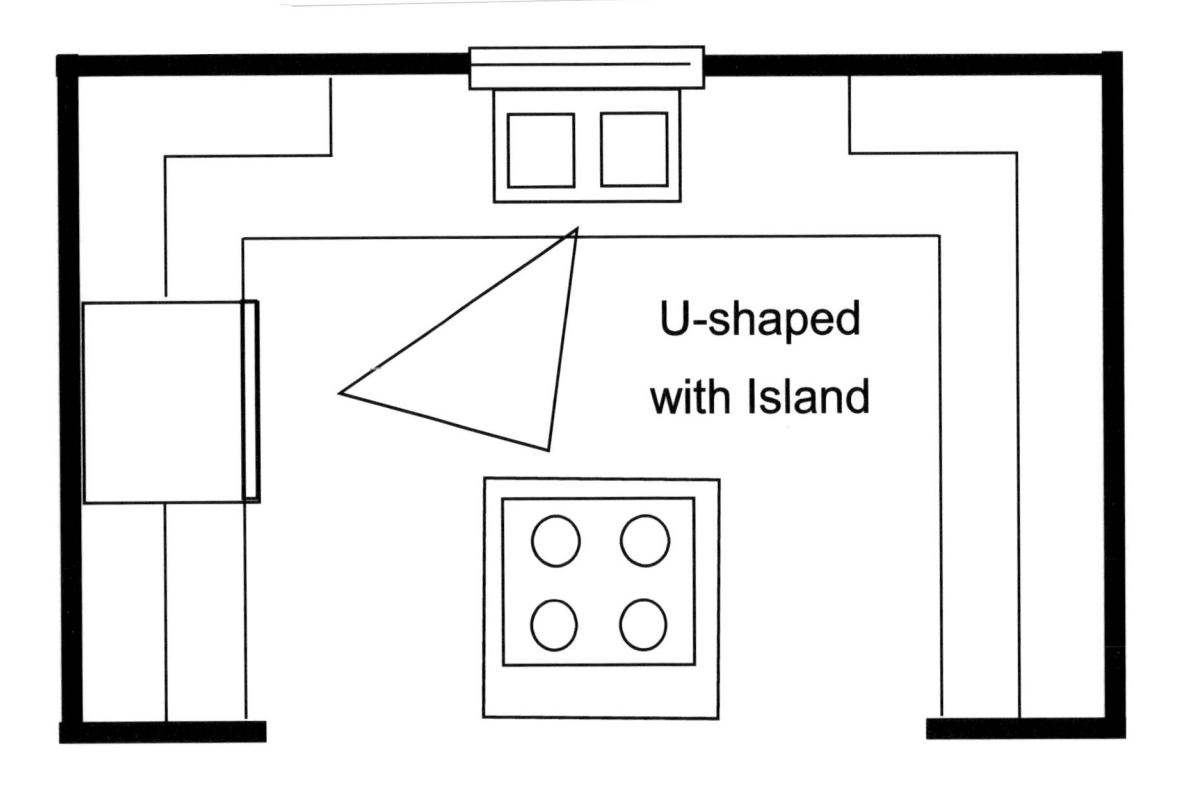

U-shaped with Island

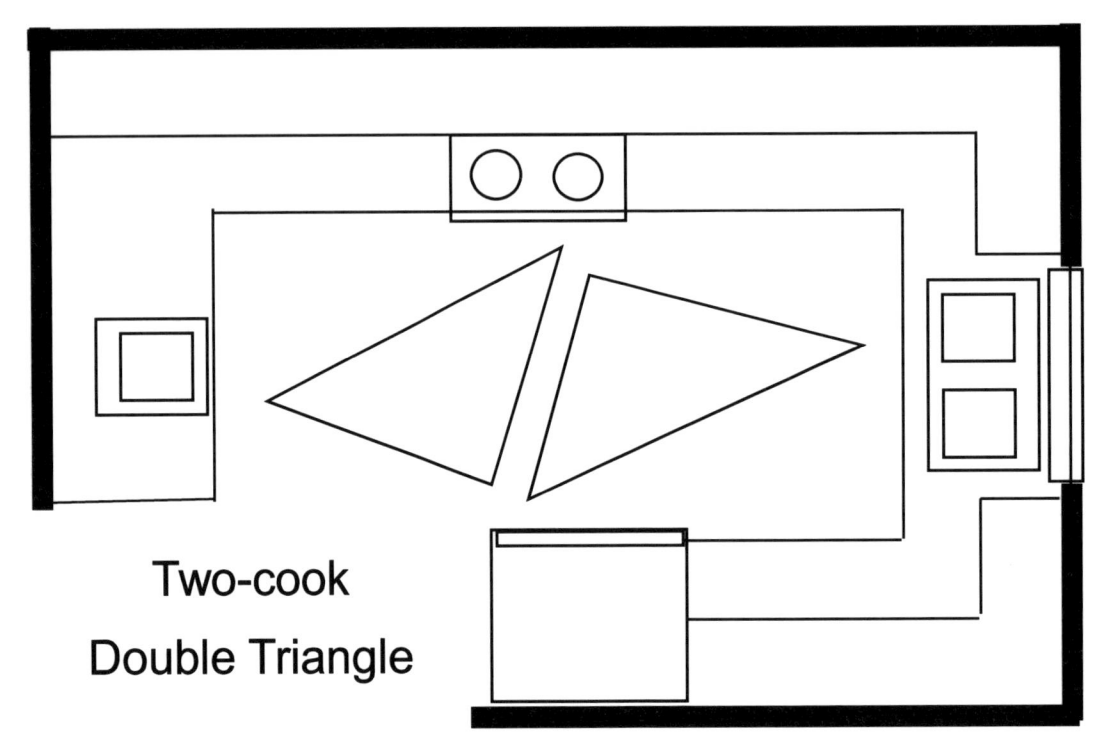

Two-cook Double Triangle

WORK TRIANGLE B

Interior Design For Today

When choosing kitchen cabinetry, factor in cost and construction quality. Kitchen cabinets are available in a variety of qualities and therefore prices. When making comparisons, consider construction details and choose those with a high standard, such as solid wood frames with doweled and glued or mortised joints. Choose solid wood drawer fronts, door frames, and doors, or solid veneered or top-grade laminate door panels.

Good quality cabinets incorporate corner braces, plywood sides, and rear panels. Adjustable shelving and pullout trays in lower cabinets are an optional benefit. Cabinet drawer sides are best if solid wood or ½-inch thick plywood with doweled or dovetailed joints rather than stapled and glued joints. Self-closing drawer, tray glides, and extension glides should have a strength resistance factor of between 75 to 100 pounds.

When designing your kitchen layout, observe typical measurements. Base cabinets are 24 inches deep by 34½ inches high. Wall cabinets are 12 to 13 inches deep and are hung at a height of roughly 18 inches above the countertop, however this height can be adjusted to suit a preference for a lower hung cabinet for better access. Any cabinetry above a range should allow 30 inches of head space. Cabinetry should be avoided over and above a sink.

Shelving & Storage

Good kitchen design incorporates maximum storage and easy assess to stored items. Placement of a closet-like pantry into the design contributes maximum use of storage space with a full-length bank of slide-out shelving for easy access. An optional pantry style is a pull-out . The addition of a "lazy-Susan" swing-out shelving provides accessible storage in corner base units.

Under-counter pull-out drawers are convenient for storage of plastics, pots and pans, or dishware. Upper cabinets typically store glassware, dinner plates, bowls, and mugs. Cutlery is stored in designated drawers with tray inserts, in close proximity to the breakfast area, while cooking utensils are stored beside the stove. Knives are frequently stored in a knife block set upon the countertop near the stove or hung onto a magnetic wall strip on the wall above the countertop. Slide out racks can be installed in lower cabinets as pot holders, tray storage, and utility storage for soaps and cleaners. To avoid countertop clutter, a built-in "appliance garage" will house the toaster, blender, mixer, coffee maker, and other small countertop appliances.

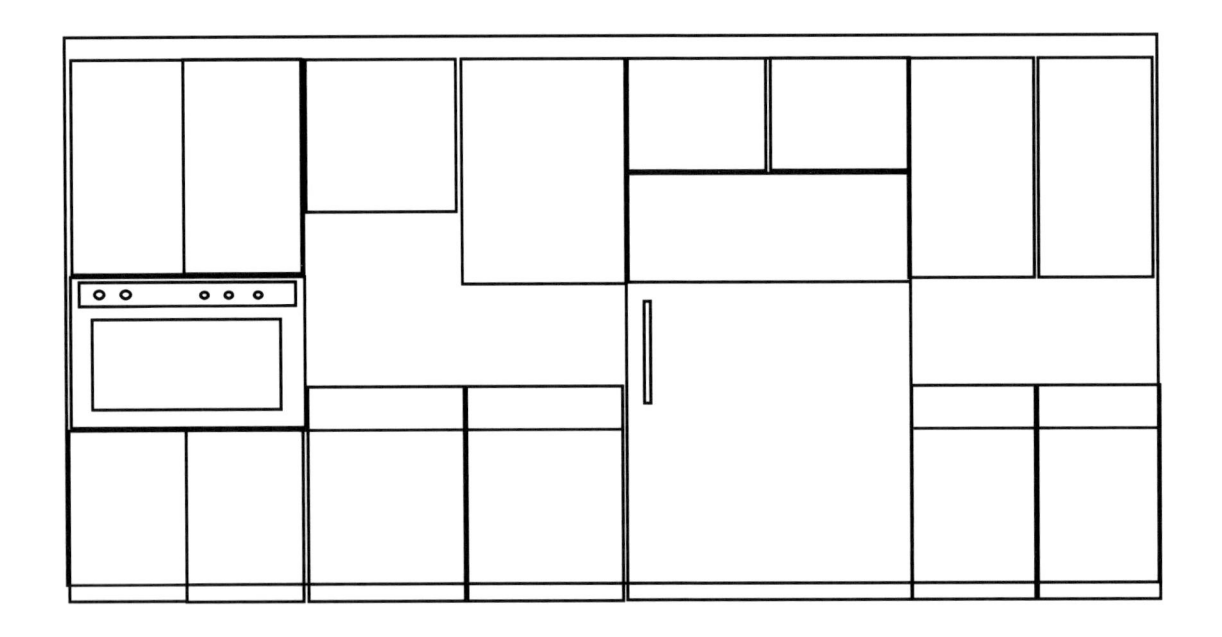

Fig. 1

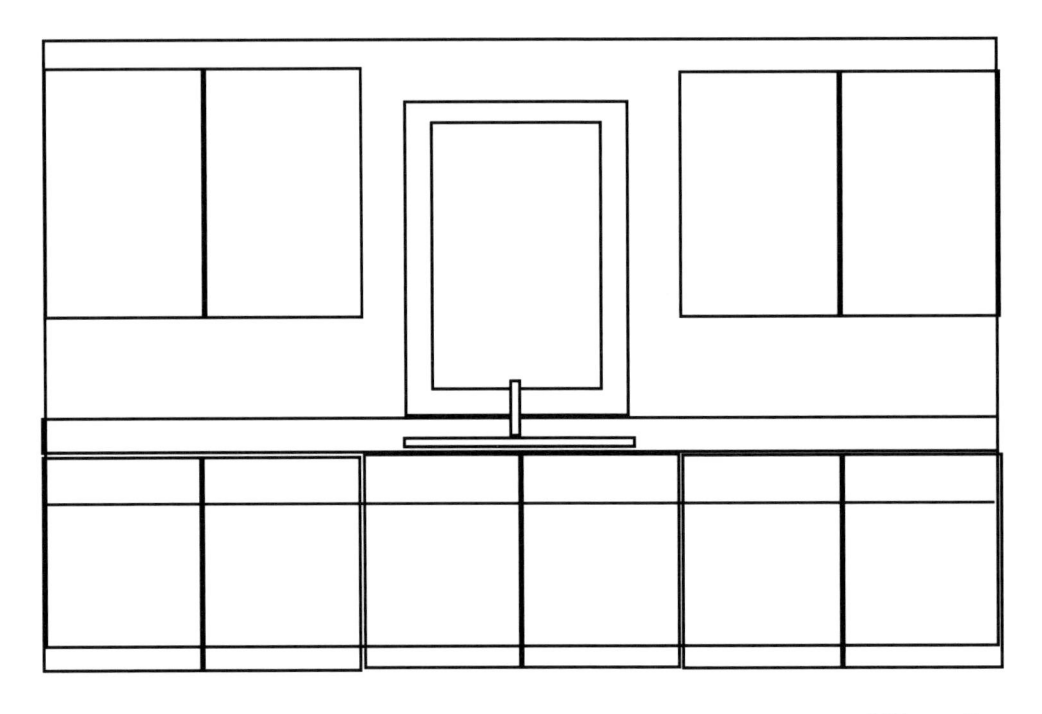

Fig. 3

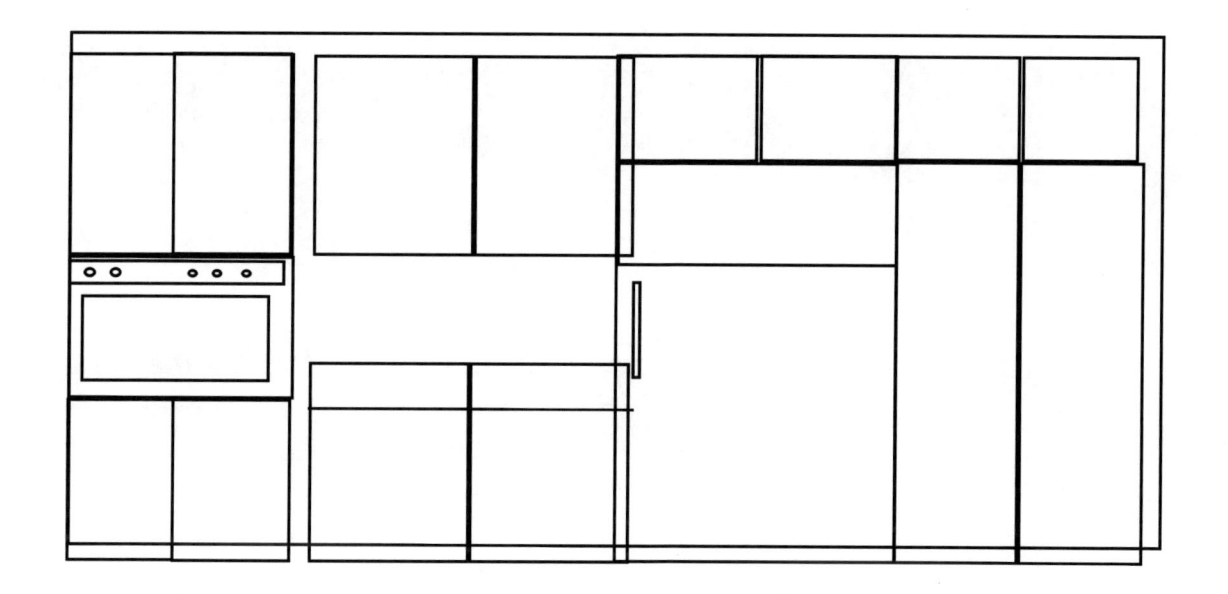

Fig. 2

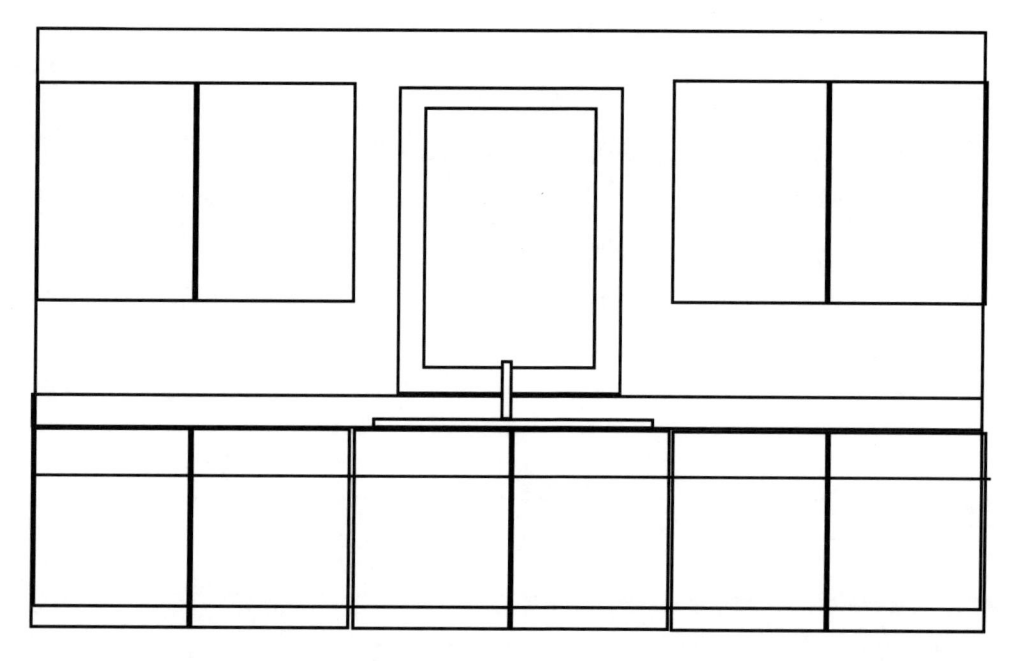

Fig. 4

KITCHEN BALANCE A

Interior Design For Today

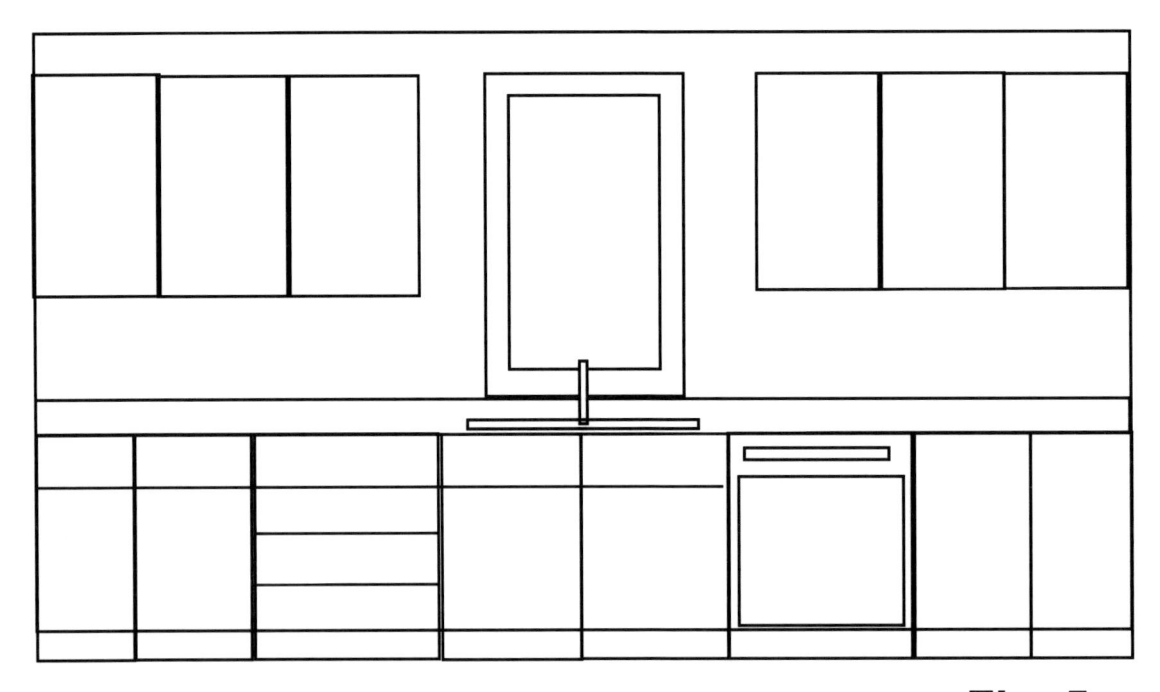

Fig. 5

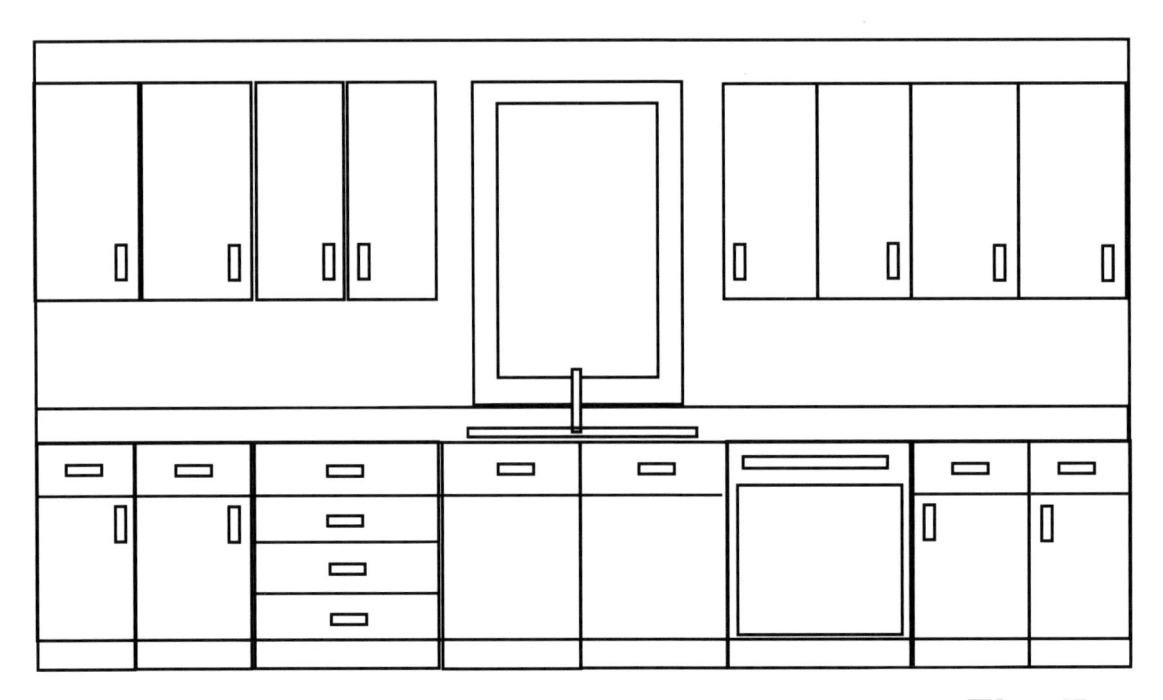

Fig. 7

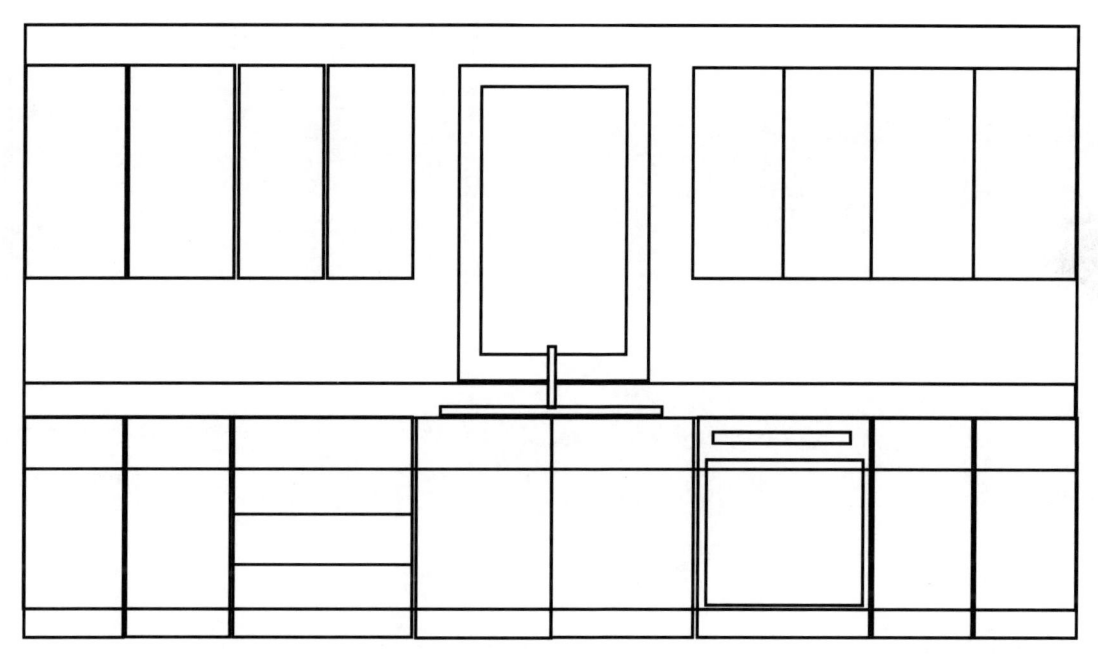

Fig. 6

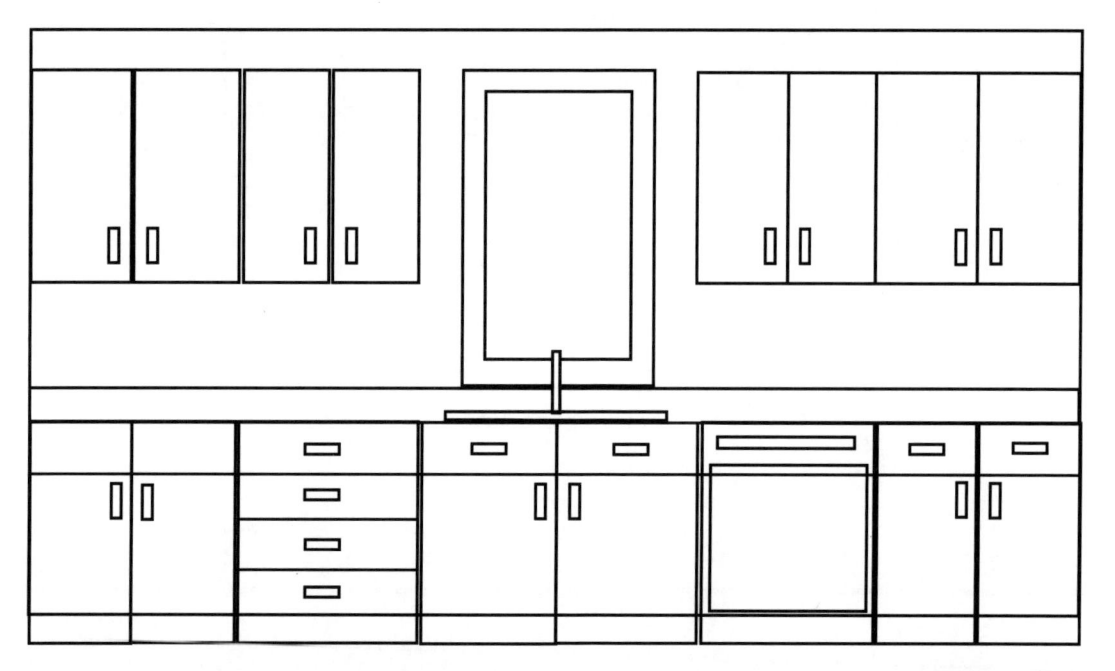

Fig. 8

KITCHEN BALANCE B

Fig. 9

Fig. 10

KITCHEN BALANCE C

Interior Design For Today

Stock, Semi-custom, & Custom Cabinetry

Cabinetry falls into three categories of construction, stock cabinetry, semi-custom cabinetry, and custom cabinetry. Each category is certified to meet guidelines for durable construction. Each category has its pros and cons and provides a choice for every budget.

Stock cabinets are pre-constructed cabinets that can be accessed through home improvement and kitchen centers. They are the most economical choice and readily available, however, they limit customizing to the space and are not constructed of solid wood.

Semi-custom cabinets are built to order. They come in a wide range of styles, colors, construction materials, and finishes, and can incorporate accessories such as storage bins, pullouts, and lazy Susans. They are more expensive than stock cabinets and have a wait on them as they are being manufactured.

Custom cabinets are built by a cabinetmaker from a choice of hardwoods such as maple, cherry, walnut, or oak. They are custom designed in that you, the designer, decides on the configuration of cabinetry to fit the kitchen. Custom cabinetry is of the best quality and the most expensive option. Its drawback is a wait of several weeks before delivery and installation.

Cabinet Measurements

Base cabinets are 24 inches deep and 34½ inches high. A standard counter top measures 1½ inches high. Combined with the base cabinet height, the total height is 36 inches. Wall cabinets are 12 to 13 inches deep and 30 to 42 inches high. In a kitchen with an 8 foot high ceiling, a 36 inch wall cabinet leaves room for a bulkhead to be framed in between the cabinet and ceiling, or for space to be left open. Cabinets installed above a refrigerator are the same depth and width as the appliance. Pantry cabinets are full-height, ranging from 84 inches high up to 96 inches high. Widths vary from 15 to 36 inches wide.

Cabinet doors should be no wider than 18 inches. Drawers can be up to 36 inches wide. Typically, when designing a kitchen, a drawer will be placed just under the countertop and above a couple of base cabinet shelves. Full banks of drawers can be added into the design, usually on either side of the range. Deep drawers are most appropriate for storing pots and pans and other cookware.

before

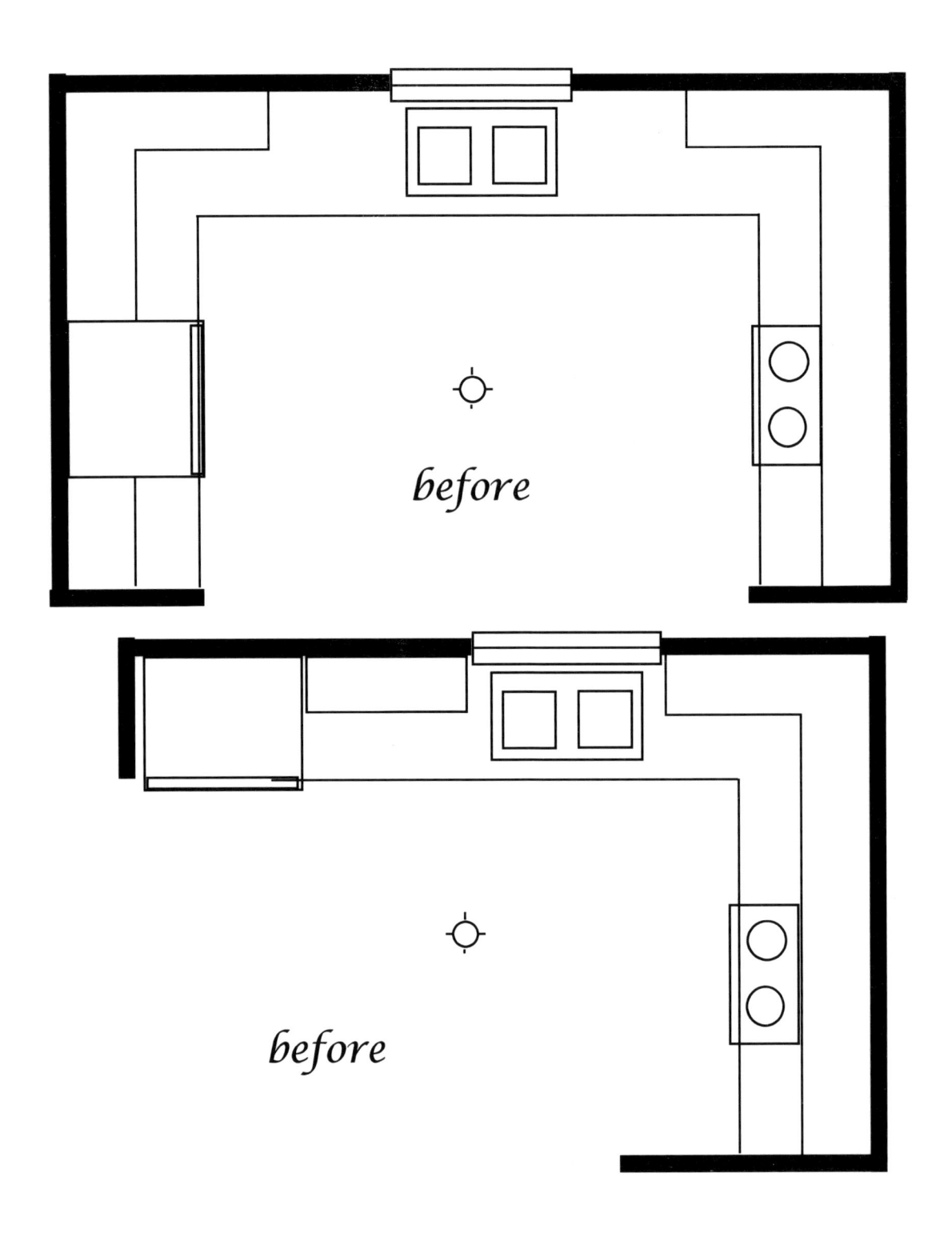

before

COUNTER SPACE & LIGHTING

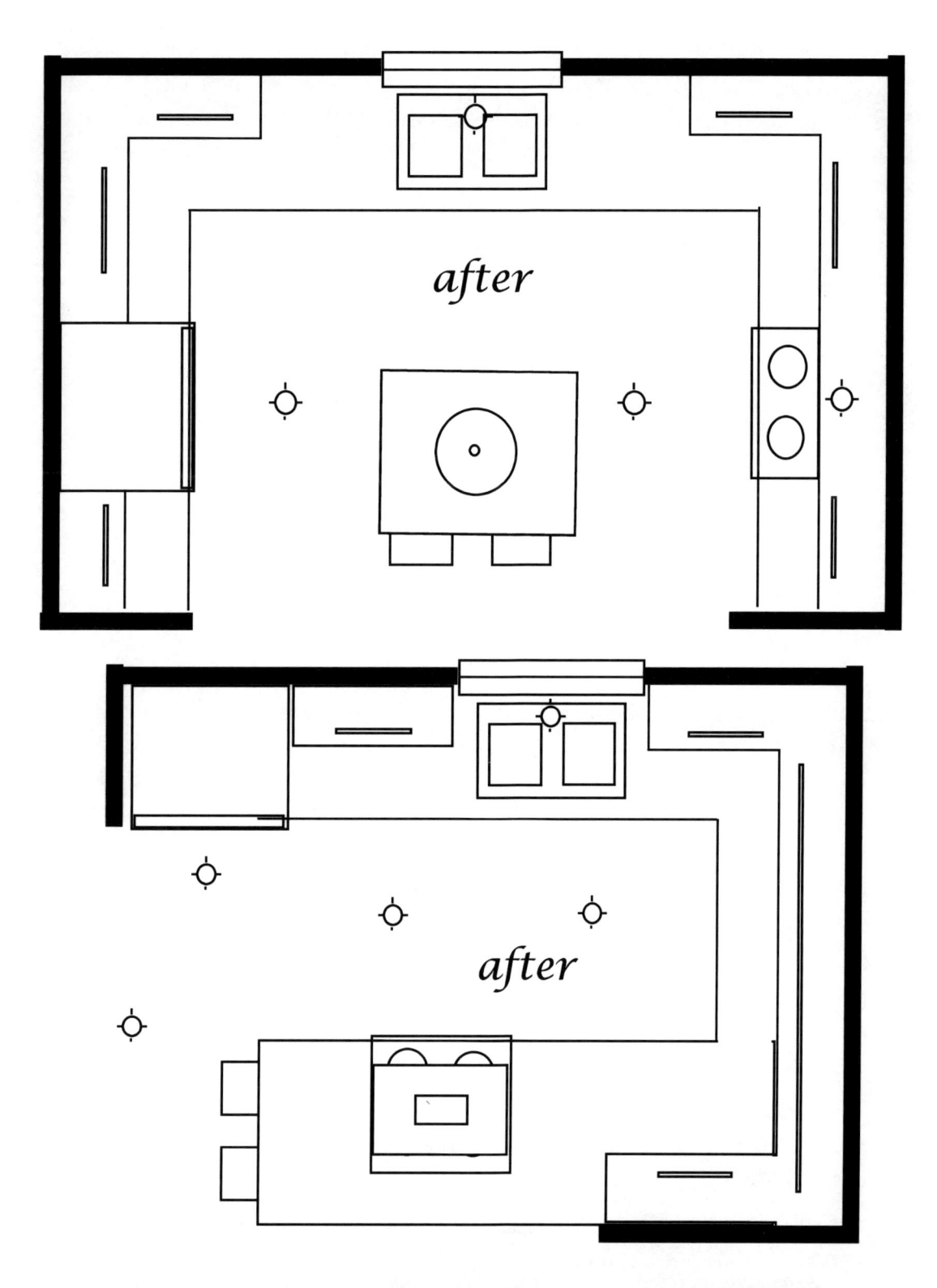

after

after

COUNTER SPACE & LIGHTING

Interior Design
For Today

A thirty-inch-high counter Island cabinetry allowing seating requires a 19 inches of leg depth and 19 inches of knee space. A 36-inch high counter requires 15 inches of leg depth and 15 inches of knee space, and a 42-inch bar counter requires 24 inches of width, 12 depth, and 12 inches of knee space.

Hardware

When choosing hardware for cabinetry, consider the architectural style reflected in its design. *Knobs*, *handles*, and *pulls* made from nickel, brass, chrome, and other forms of steel, porcelain, ceramic, glass, and wood, are available in a variety of designs. Choose hardware in-keeping with the style of the kitchen cabinetry. If the kitchen has a clean, sleek, modern look, invisible hardware, or a bolder stainless steel rod handle will fit, while a more traditional kitchen will require more decorative hardware.

Countertops

Natural materials as well as laminate synthetic materials qualify as durable, hard-wearing countertop surfaces. *Laminate* countertop is constructed of 3/4-inch thick plywood or particleboard with a 1/16-inch polymer layer bonded to it. It is durable, stain-resistant, and cleans easily, however needs protection from hot pans and sharp knives. For a longer-wearing laminate surface, the color is mixed with the polymer, and if chipped or scratched, prevents the undersurface from showing through.

Laminate countertop edges are flush-trimmed, or beveled. For a less custom-look finish, laminate is available with a pre-fixed rolled front edge and attached backsplash. Laminate comes in a variety of colors, textures, and patterns, and fits any decor style.

Solid-surfacing is a choice for countertops made from 1/4 to 11/2-inch thick synthetic material to resemble stone and known by the most well-known trade name of "Corian."

Solid surfacing is non-porous and very durable, however hot pots and knives can scratch and burn it. It comes in a display of colors and patterns to suit a variety of decors.

Natural stone surfacing such as granite, marble, and soapstone, is extremely expensive, but a very popular kitchen countertop choice where cost is not a concern and a tough, but elegant maintenance-free surface is. It is available in varying thicknesses and qualities with various decorative edge treatments. It is durable, cleans easily, resists scratching, and has a gleaming, smooth surface that reflects light and bounces it around the room. One drawback to stone as a countertop material, is its porosity requiring periodic sealing as well as its lack of color and pattern choices.

Concrete is a custom countertop material poured at the site in a seamless slab. This surface is durable when sealed to protect its color as well as making it stain-resistant. Because of its industrial look and feel, it suits a very contemporary style kitchen.

Stainless steel is durable, easy to clean, and has a commercial look and feel to it. It is a choice for modern and contemporary kitchens.

Sinks

Kitchen sinks are available in 6-8-inch depths and in an array of sizes and materials to suit any style and budget.

Stainless steel is the most popular sink which comes in a variety of configurations, some with one basin, others with two, others with three. It is easy to clean, chip-resistant, and comes in either a matte or shiny finish. The thickness of its steel is rated as 18-gauge or 20-gauge, 18-gauge being the thicker and more durable.

Sinks are also available in composite materials mixed with an acrylic or polyester-resin base and known as "solid-surface." Undermount installations are integrated with a solid-surface countertop.

Other sink materials available include cast iron, vitreous china, and acrylic composites.

Faucets

Choosing a faucet for the kitchen sink requires an informed decision, as faucets fill function, but also add style. Choose from single-handled disk-type faucets which are the most durable, single or double handled cartridge-type faucets, or single-handled ball-type faucets in a variety of styles. Choose a "gooseneck" faucet or one with a retractable or pullout spray head for extra convenience.

Appliances

When considering kitchen appliances, the choice between gas and electric needs to be established. Gas cook tops and ranges provide instant heat, however, unless their burners are sealed, clean-up is difficult. An electric range, or cooktop, on the other hand, with a smooth glass-ceramic surface, is easy to clean and sleek-looking.

Convection ovens which circulate heat and produce even heat outweighs a thermal oven which depends on heat elements on the top and bottom of the unit. Self-cleaning, electronic controls, and professional styling are all available in today's ranges and bring impact to the work station.

Wall ovens are a practical and attractive alternative to the range oven. When positioning a wall oven, place it at a convenient height, usually at countertop level, or place double ovens one above the other. Another arrangement, is to build in a microwave oven above the wall oven. Consider convenience in the work triangle and take into consideration the opening of the microwave door outward from the work triangle.

When planning your kitchen around the installation of a range, venting needs to be addressed. Updraft venting is installed at a height above the stove and vented out through the wall, therefore, when positioning a range, it needs to back onto an outside wall. This venting option allows for the use of a decorative range hood.

Another venting option is the down-draft system where the vent is built-into the cooktop and pulls air down and out through an outside wall.

A self-venting hood which only filters and re-circulates air is an inexpensive option that should only be considered on a low-budget kitchen up-date and should not be considered for a new kitchen.

The refrigerator should be placed at the end of a bank of cabinets allowing for the most uninterrupted stretch of countertop with the door opening away from the work triangle. The choice in refrigerator will be determined by the capacity needed and the budget. Freestanding and built-in models are available in a selection of colors. As a general rule, refrigerators should match in color and style with that of other appliances. If your built-in trim kit allows installation of door panels, these should co-ordinate with the kitchen cabinetry and other built in appliances.

Other appliances to be considered for the kitchen design is a dishwasher, garbage disposal unit, and hot water dispenser.

Use Solid Surface Countertops

Windows, Lighting & Electrical

A kitchen requires maximum lighting whether from natural sunlight or artificial light. When arranging the kitchen layout, a good place to position a sink is under a window for natural daylight. The sink should be centered under the window for balance. When considering a window treatment, cleanability and fire-resistance are factors. Blinds are the best choice to allow the most light and keep an uncluttered clean-line look.

For attractive ambient lighting, downlighting with halogen potlights staggered throughout the kitchen ceiling is a good choice. Functional task lighting over the sink can also be supplied with downlights. Task lighting over a cooktop is supplied by built-in lighting in the exhaust hood, while installation of undercounter lighting provides lighting for countertops. If an island or peninsula is in the design, hanging pendant lamps over this area of countertop are appropriate. Refer back to COUNTER SPACE & LIGHTING for help.

Placement of switches should be functional, but also provide independent control over each form of lighting for most flexibility. Dimmer switches on pot lights also contribute to flexibility.

In kitchen design, placement of electrical outlets are of great importance. Make sure outlets are placed above the counter tops for appliances. A qualified electrician will know how to wire large appliances, including the refrigerator, range, dishwasher, and microwave on their own circuits. However you are responsible to see that placement of outlets are precisely where they are needed.

Flooring

Kitchen flooring should be hard-wearing, water-resistant, easy to clean, and durable. Choices include vinyl, linoleum, ceramic tile, stone, hardwood, cork, and laminate.

Vinyl is an affordable choice in kitchen flooring. It is low maintenance, comfortable underfoot, and comes in a variety of colors and patterns. Vinyl's drawback is that is can be damaged with burns and sharp objects.

Linoleum is harder than vinyl and more durable. It doesn't show scuffs and scratches and is easy to clean. Linoleum, however, is put down in tiles with seam lines that can catch dirt and trap moisture. Another drawback to linoleum is its need to be waxed to keep its finish polished.

Ceramic tile comes in various shapes and sizes, textures, and durability, glazed or unglazed. It resists moisture and stains. Although ceramic tile looks great and helps to upgrade the appearance of any kitchen, it is cold underfoot unless heating is installed under the tile and its hard surface makes it uncomfortable to walk on for long lengths of time.

Stone tile, including granite, marble, and slate, and manufactured quartz, is indestructible, therefore long-lasting. Stone needs periodic sealing to prevent moisture absorption.

Hardwoods, including oak, birch, cherry, maple, hickory, and walnut, as well as imported varieties such as mahogany and teak, are warm and beautiful, however, water damage is a concern and therefore not a popular choice.

Cork tile simulates the look of burled hardwood and comes in a variety of stains. It is cushiony and comfortable underfoot, resists moisture, cleans easily, and is durable, however, cork flooring needs to be sanded and refinished every few years to keep its surface in good repair.

Plastic laminate flooring is easy to clean and durable, and is available in a multitude of wood-like and ceramic-like finishes. However, laminate will scratch and dent.

OUR HOUSE A HOME

Add Modern Touches

Designing a Bathroom

Questionnaire

When designing a bathroom, filling out a preliminary questionnaire will help you to understand your client's preferences. Have your client gather pictures from magazines or bath centers. These will help you to pin-point exactly what style your client is leaning toward as well as mood and color preferences. Refer to the BATHROOM QUESTIONNAIRE.

Take note of positive features in the room, such as natural light, and note any problem features. Your job will be to accentuate the positive and eliminate or camouflage the negative.

Note functional needs expressed by the client. Does the client want a tub, or will a shower suffice? If a tub, is your client's preference a whirlpool tub? Are both a shower and tub required?

Consider space and privacy for the people who may share the bathroom at the same time. Is there need for a large counter space and more than one sink?

Important to consider when planning out the bathroom space are a private zone for the toilet, and smooth flow of traffic without obstruction by doors. If there is not sufficient lighting, especially task lighting, it will have to be allowed for, as well sufficient storage for towels and toiletries. It is also at the planning stage that any home entertainment components will be incorporated into the design according to the wishes of the client.

Bathroom Style

As with any other room, the mood will need to be determined. Will it be contemporary or traditional, warm, or cool, cozy or sleek? Warm, earthy, natural, and muted tones are most flattering to the face, so choosing from a subdued palette will be appropriate if the bathroom is the main dressing and make-up area. All elements will need to work together and be appropriate for the size or room. Refer to BATHROOM VINTAGE or MODERN.

BATHROOM DESIGN QUESTIONNAIRE

CLIENT:_____

HOME ADDRESS:_____

JOB LOCATION:_____

DATE:

PHONE: **SCOPE OF JOB:**

- How many adults will be using the bathroom? How many children? What are their ages?

_____

_____

- What fixtures are present in this bathroom? What fixtures do you want to add?

_____

_____

- Are you planning any structural changes? If so, describe them.

_____

_____

- Where is the bathroom located, in the basement, on the first, or on the second floor? What is beneath and above it?

_____

_____

- Is there heating ductwork in the walls?

_____

- What is the rating of the electrical service?

_____

- Can present doors and windows be relocated?

_____

- What lighting fixtures do you prefer, downlights or wall-mounted fixtures?
  _____
  _____

- What are your storage requirements?
  _____
  _____

- What color combinations do you like? What fixture color do you prefer?
  _____
  _____

- What are your preferences regarding cabinet and countertop material?
  _____
  _____

- What is your flooring preference?
  _____
  _____

- What are your wall treatment preferences?
  _____
  _____

- What framework of time do you have for completion?
  _____
  _____

- What is your budget?
  _____
  _____

Interior Design For Today

Design Your Space Appropriately

Scope of the Job

A simple redecoration does not require structural change, nor does it encompass moving plumbing. In such a case, the main changes might include new fixtures, faucets, paint, mirrors, window treatments, flooring material, and storage. If the scope of the job entails renovation where structural changes will be made, or the location of fixtures will be changed, a a plumber, electrician, and general contractor will need to be involved. A Building Permit, which is the responsibility of the general contractor, may be required to meet the Building Code. With a structural overhaul entailing the removal of walls between the bathroom and other adjacent rooms to incorporate their space, the expertise of an architect may also be needed.

Basic Layouts

The 2-piece **Powder Room** consists of a sink and toilet. Its dimensions can fit a minimum space of 4' x 4' 6" or 3' x 6." This bathroom preferably opens off a hallway that is located near the front or back entrance, or near the living room of a home for easy access by guests. Because it is less private and more visual than other bathrooms, it may be sound-proofed and treated with more aesthetically pleasing decor. Refer to SAMPLE BATHROOM LAYOUTS A for basic samples to be expanded upon as space is available.

The ***Family Bathroom*** is one of the most used bathrooms and needs to be outfitted with the most durable fixtures and easy to clean finishes. It consists of a sink, toilet, and bathtub or tub/shower combination. The minimum space required for a family bathroom is 5' x 7.'

Fixtures set into separate compartments facilitate the use of this bathroom by more than one family member at a time without interference. This can be accommodated into the design if the space is large enough. See the basic *11' 6" x 8' Family Bathroom* on SAMPLE BATHROOM LAYOUTS A. The toilet and tub are separated from the sink and grooming area. A ***Children's Bathroom*** is often a shared facility between two or more children. It is important to "compartmentalize" this bathroom, separating the toilet and bathing areas from the sinks and grooming area. See the basic *12' 6" x 6' Children's Bathroom* sample on your help.

Special considerations of the children's bathroom are slip-resistant flooring, durable countertops and cabinets, single-control faucets to minimize hot water burns, as well as efficient and compartmentalized storage for each child. This bathroom should be located for easy access in the bedroom wing of the house.

4' X 5'

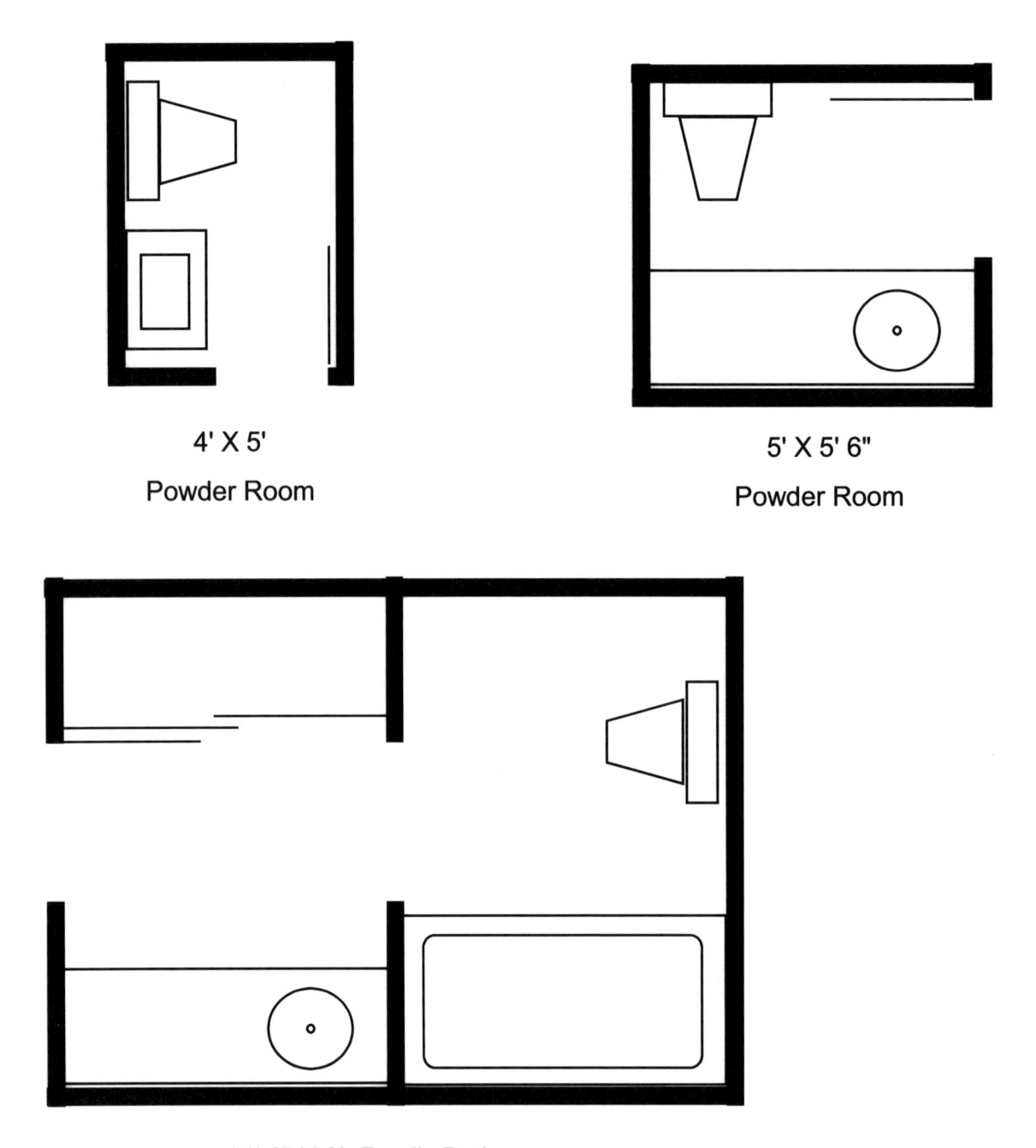

Powder Room

5' X 5' 6"

Powder Room

11' 6" X 8' Family Bathroom

SAMPLE BATHROOM LAYOUTS A

Interior Design For Today

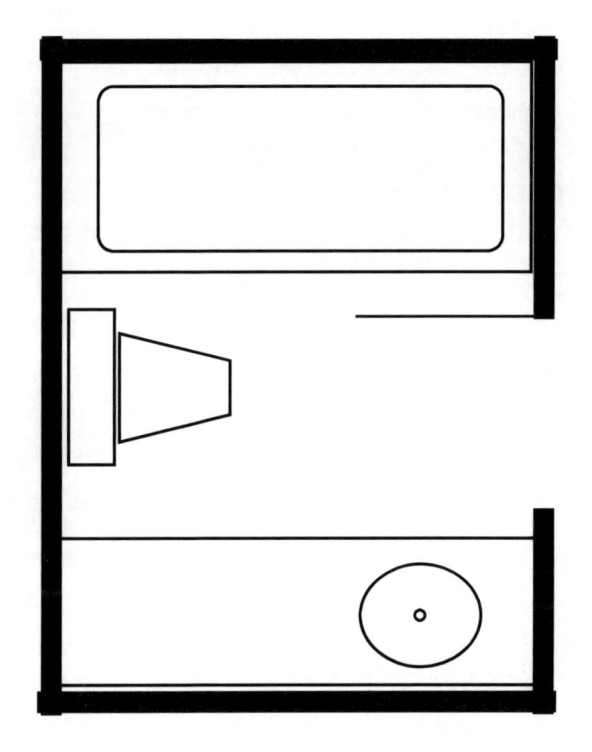

5' 6" X 8' Family Bathroom

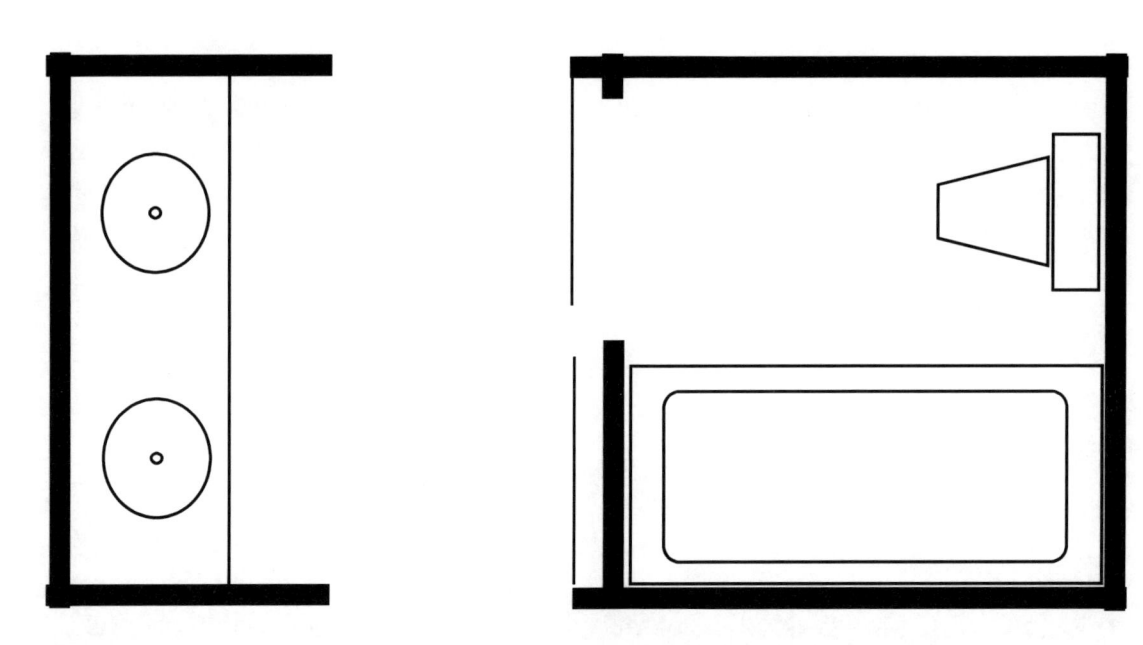

12' 6" X 6' Children's Bathroom

SAMPLE BATHROOM LAYOUTS A

Interior Design For Today

The **Master Bathroom**, or "Ensuite" is the most highly personalized and indulgent bathroom. It not just facilitates utilitarian functions, but provide a luxurious space to relax, as well as incorporates amenities suiting the interests of its owners. It will include toilet, tub, shower, sinks, and grooming areas, but also, as space permits, may include a make-up center, walk-in-closet, entertainment center including a TV, VCR, or sound system, a fireplace, a sauna, a spa, or a gym.

The Master Bathroom, because of its source of pleasure, will be decked out in the latest gadgetry. A separate soaker or whirlpool tub with "Roman" or "Waterfall" deck or wall-mounted spouts replaces the standard bathtub while

a large walk-in shower with multiple, adjustable surround multijet shower fittings with equalized pressure and water temperature controls replace the tub surround. Refer to the SAMPLE BATHROOM LAYOUT B help to see how a basic master bathroom can be laid out.

Basic Plumbing

Fixtures, including toilet, bathtub, sink, shower stall, and fittings, including faucets, showerheads, knobs, drains, and visible pipes, are the basic plumbing elements. Every bathroom fixture has cold and hot water supply pipes and a drain pipe to drain away waste water. Every drain has a trap where water is caught to prevent noxious sewer gas back-up into the house. Every drain system has a vent stack into which bathroom fixtures are tied. This pipe goes up above the building and allows air in and gasses out. You will need to be familiar with these basics when designing or redesigning a bathroom space.

Fixtures

A variety of different-styled sinks is available, including deck-mounted, integral-bowl, pedestal, wall-hung, and vessel. Tubs can be freestanding, pedestal, or built-in, soaking or whirlpool. Innovative vacuum-formed acrylic or injection-molded thermoplastic tubs are available in neutrals and the latest colors. Popular today is the walk-in tiled shower with multiple shower heads and solid glass door. To allow maximum natural lighting into the shower area, the use of glass or glass block wall is employed. Choose between a traditional two-piece toilet and a European-styled "low-boy" one-piece design.

Faucets

Faucets are popular in polished chrome, brushed chrome, and brushed nickel, with single, center-set, or spread-fit controls that are either sink-mounted, deck-mounted, or wall-mounted. Familiarize yourself with what is available from suppliers of bathroom fixtures.

Countertops

Plastic laminate and solid-surface acrylic countertops are most popular bathroom surfaces, however others are available, including stone, glass, and synthetic marble.

Plastic laminate is durable, water resistant, easy to clean, and relatively inexpensive.

Solid-surface materials are durable, heat resistant, easy to clean, water resistant, and can be shaped to fit a variety of styles and forms. It is also conducive to integral sink installation providing a clean, sleek, look.

Storage

Storage is a necessary component of the bathroom design. Choose traditional designs from free-standing furniture-like cabinetry to sleek, modern built-in designs. If space permits, a built-in closet that houses towels and toiletries is a big bonus.

Floors

The most popular bathroom flooring choice is ceramic tile. It is tough, durable, water-resistant, maintenance free, and attractive with a wide range of textures, patterns, colors, shapes, and finishes to choose from. However, there are some disadvantages to ceramic tile. It is cold underfoot unless heated, slippery when wet, and unless grout lines are sealed, they are susceptible to mildew.

An optional choice in bathroom flooring is vinyl which is resilient, moisture resistant, and available in a variety of colors, textures, and patterns. The disadvantage of vinyl flooring is its vulnerability to dents and tears.

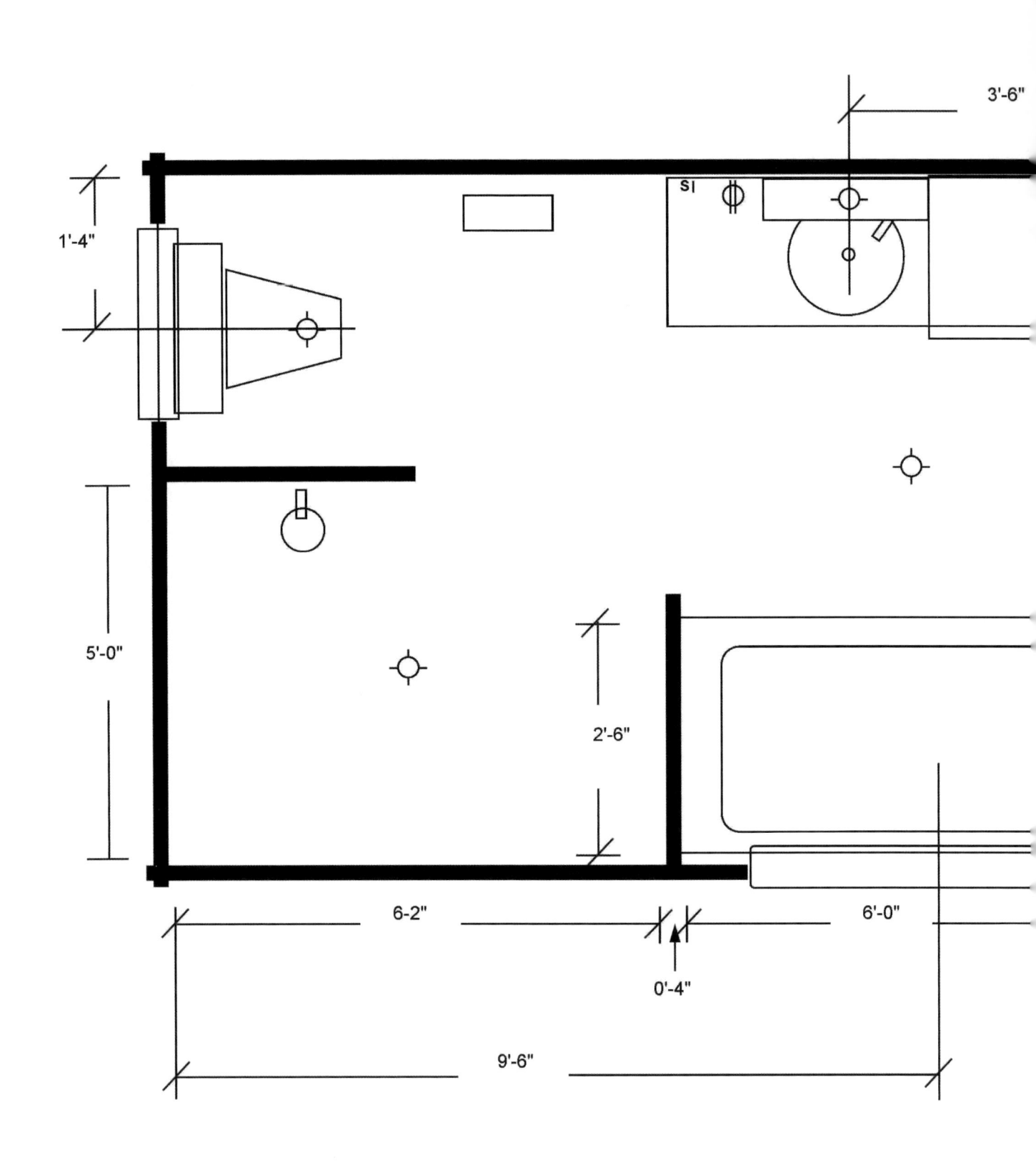

SAMPLE BATHROOM LAYOUT B

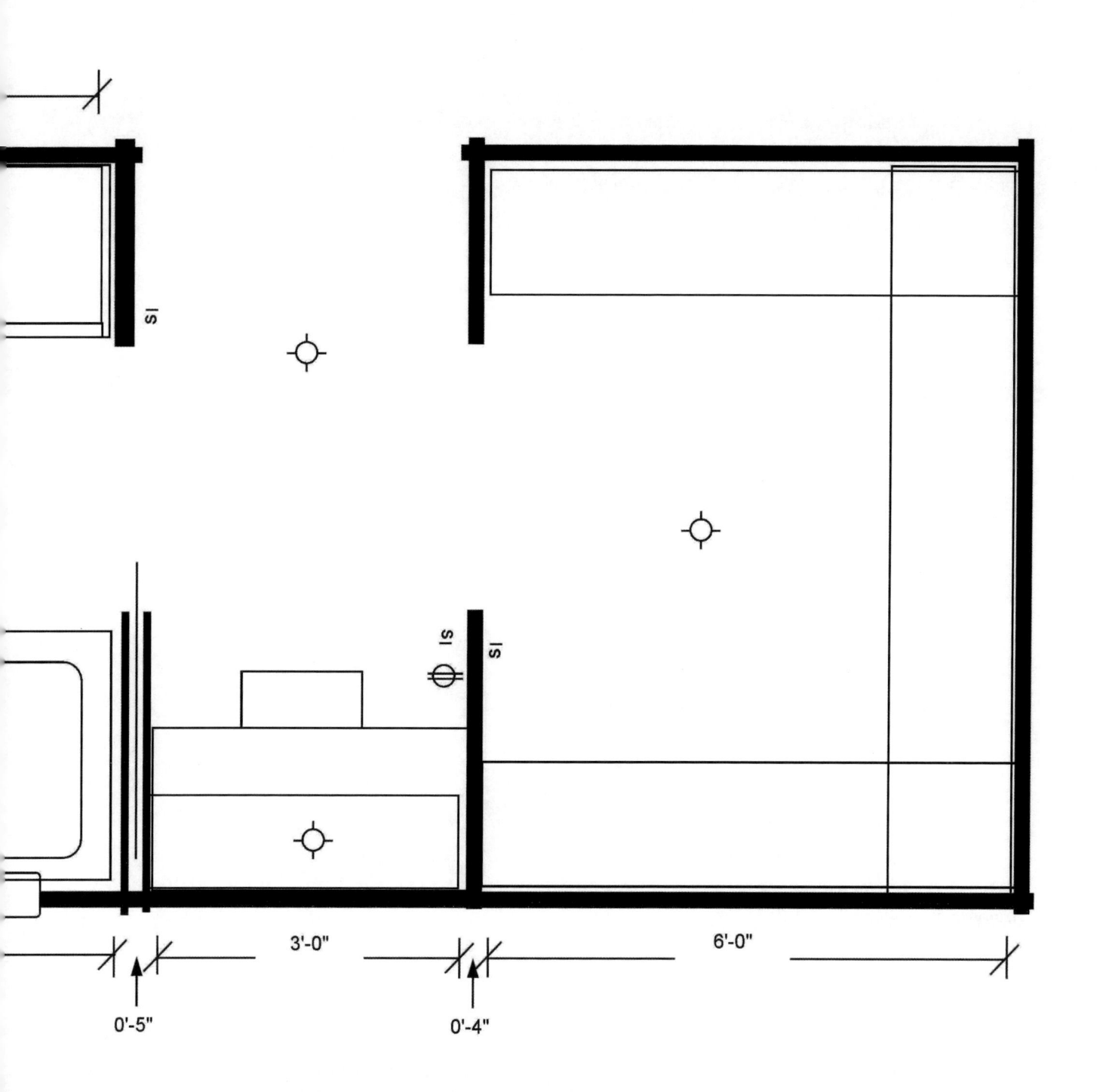

Master Bathroom with Grooming Area
and Walk-in Closet

Interior Design
For Today

Walls

Suitable wall paint for bathrooms includes either water-based latex or oil-based alkyd in a satin finish. Any durable, scrubable, stain resistant, vinyl wallpaper is appropriate for bathroom use.

Glazed wall tile is used to cover wall areas around the bathtub and sink. Typical 3 x 3 inch, 4¼ x 4¼ inch, and 6 x 6 inch wall tile can be punched-up with a row of small decorative tile as an accent. Because it is completely impervious to water, vitreous tile is best used in the shower.

Lighting

Built-in downlighting is appropriate for general lighting, as well as for lighting in specific areas of a bathroom such as over a toilet, and in the shower. Special waterproof shower lighting fixture units with neoprene seals are available.

Task lighting is reserved for over a sink and mirror. This form of lighting can be accomplished with a wall light fixture above the mirror, wall sconces flanking the mirror, or with a bulkhead and potlights above the sink and mirror.

Heating and Ventilation

Add a bathroom heater, an auxiliary heater, or wall or ceiling heater with a thermostat, timer, and safety cutoff to pre-warm a bathroom. Another option to keep a bathroom warm and dry is to install a heated towel bar, either water-powered or electric. Always install an exhaust fan.

Accessories

When the bathroom is completed, and it is time for the finishing touches, towel bars, hooks, soap dishes, toothbrush holders, cup holders, and adjustable mirrors are added to give pizzaz and a touch of luxury. Research various styles available and add these items to your bathroom scheme according to the style preferences of your client.

Use Hard-wearing Surfaces

The Interior Design Project

*I*n putting an **Interior Design Project** together, you will want to assess the project and come up with a time and work schedule. Your approach will be determined by the **Scope of the Job**. You will need to consider if the project is a complete overhaul of a space where there is free reign to bring in a completely new look along with new furnishings and decoration, if it is a partial re-do, or a re-design in which a client's furnishings are kept and recycled within the scheme. In this lesson you will learn how to assess your project and schedule it so that the job will run smoothly without upsets or delays.

Scope of the Job

Assessing the Job

In determining the scope of the job, you will need to assess the rooms you are working on, asking yourself, "what is the starting point?" Is the home new and requiring only the application of new furnishings and decoration, or is it an older home requiring laborious stripping of layered wallpaper, needing re-plastering, new trims and baseboards, and new flooring, as well as complete decoration, or does the job entail only a face-lift and re-arrangement of existing furnishings?

Working with the Trades

If more than just a face-lift, or a "staging" is required, you will need to enlist the services of trades people. Begin your preparations well in advance. Make up a schedule and contact trades people in your area whom you can rely on to do the work. Be sure to prioritize your list of jobs in the order in which they will take place.

Before trades people will agree to the project, a working drawing of the floorplan will be required. Your responsibility is to prepare to-scale drawings for your trades people. However, if the job entails a complete renovation, an engineered drawing may be required.

If your project is in an older home, you will have to be very particular about the detail of operation. Once all the furnishings, window coverings, and if the floors are being replaced, old flooring is removed from the room, the woodwork, if needing replacement, will have to be removed. This job will require the expertise of a contractor or home renovator. Next, the condition of the walls will need to be addressed. If they are wallpapered, wallpaper will need to be stripped and holes patched. This job will require a plasterer if the walls are in need of a skim coat. If only minor fixes are needed, your painter will be able to handle this in preparation for paint.

Any electrical wiring for lighting will be installed next and your electrician will already have been booked in advance so that he is available at this time when you need his services to rough it in.

Once the wiring is completed, your painter will be able to prepare the walls for paint. If your contract entails a kitchen or bathroom remodel, plumbing will need to be installed at this point.

Once walls are painted, and any scheduled wallpapering is done, your carpenter will be able to install and paint out any new trim, mouldings, baseboard, and interior doors, adding pre-selected hardware as needed.

The next scheduled job is to look after floor treatments. If hardwood, ceramic tile, or any other hard surface flooring is scheduled in, it is at this point that it can be installed as well as wall-to-wall carpeting.

Built-ins, kitchen and bathroom cabinetry, fixtures, and faucets are next on the list. The electrician is called in again to finish his job of capping downlights, hanging ceiling fixtures, mounting wall fixtures, and covering switches and receptacles with plates.

Bathroom mirrors, towel bars and hooks, glass shelving, toilet paper holders, and any other wall mount accessories can now be installed. Window treatments are hung, and furnishings and area rugs are brought in and arranged. Final touches are added in bed treatments and accessories.

Finishing Touches

Hanging Light Fixtures

When choosing a dining room fixture, its size is important, as well as its drop. The fixture's diameter should measure one-third the length of the table, and hang 30 to 34 inches above the table or 60 - 64 inches from the floor. It should drop centered over the table. For a more contemporary look, hang two or three smaller fixtures in a row over a rectangular table instead of a single fixture.

Placing Lamps

When placing lamps, consider their purpose. If their lighting is used for reading, the bottom of the lampshade should be at eye level when sitting up. When a floor lamp is used, and its lampshade is taller than eye level, place it 10 inches further back so that there is no direct glare.

Bedroom lamps are adjusted so that the bottom of lampshades are at shoulder height when sitting in bed.

Placing Area Rugs

Several guidelines apply when choosing and laying an area rug. The rug is to be in proportion to the space. If the room is rectangular, the area rug will be rectangular. If the space is square, the rug will be square. Ideally, an equal amount of space is left uncovered around the edges of the room.

An area rug should reach under all or most of the seating arrangement in a living room with no more than two feet of empty rug beyond the furniture. Back legs of a sofa need not be on carpet, and a pleasant rug arrangement can be accomplished by adjusting the sofa to fit.

A dining room area rug should extend 18-24 inches past the edges of the table to properly accommodate pulled out chairs.

If a bed is not centered in a bedroom, use two or three smaller rugs around the bed rather than one large area rug for better balance.

Hanging Pictures

Accessorize your room with artwork. When hanging pictures, group them with other furnishings unless they are of large enough proportion to stand alone.

Ground artwork and pictures in proportion to their size. Hang artwork above a sofa, over a small table, or above a chair. Keep the center of all pictures in the room at 60 inches from the floor. When combining pictures into a display grouping, treat their arrangement as a whole and center it at 60 inches from the floor. Space pictures 3 - 4 inches apart and keep frames and matting color-matched for a flowing coherent look. Use restraint when accessorizing with artwork and avoid competition with other displays in the room for more impact.

Add decorative accessories in the form of bowls, vases, plates, baskets, etc., as well as throws and accent pillows, all color and style co-ordinated with the room. Refer to ACCESSORIES.

ACCESSORIES

Interior Design For Today

© Copyright 2013

Re-design and Staging

S*taging*, which incorporates ***re-design*** to set the stage in preparation to "show a home," is becoming a popular profession. In this lesson, you will become familiar with a stager's perspective on design. Because staging includes the overall re-design of a complete home, the emphasis is on unity and harmony of mood and style throughout. You will be able to apply rules and principles of design already taught with Interior Design, however, your eye will be trained to also apply these rules throughout the space using a client's own furnishings instead of beginning with a clean slate.

"Keep It Uncluttered"

Working with a Client

Room Condition Check List

You have been asked to take on a staging job. With clip board in hand and a copy of a Room Condition Check List, begin filling in information regarding the condition of rooms to be considered for re-design as you walk through the home.

First, make note of the paint condition of interior walls. Do walls need re-painting, or are they presentable? Look for neutral wall colors. If the rooms are bold-colored, these may need to be toned down, however, if rooms are large enough to handle the color, harmony between rooms can be accomplished by using a fresh neutral hue throughout transitional areas of the home including entranceways and hallways. If, however, re-painting is needed, a continuous neutral color throughout is the best choice.

Choosing A Color Palette

When re-designing or staging a room, a co-ordinated paint palette is as important as with any Interior Design project and must be considered with care. The paint palette can be drawn from existing fabric colors within the room and the most expensive item will be considered first.

In the living room, for instance, the sofa would qualify to have its color, or combination of colors drawn out to contribute to a color palette for the room. However, the condition of the sofa will have to be taken into consideration. Is it in good condition, is it presentable, or does it need to be replaced or covered? Make note of its condition on your Room Condition Check List.

The next consideration is the color of the sofa. What are the colors in it? Is the color neutral, that is, is it white, black, beige, brown, or gray? If so, unless a monochromatic color palette is used in the room, a second item in the room will need to be considered to draw color for the palette. Is there an interesting and in good condition area rug or drapery fabric from which color can be drawn? If so, one of these might be employed.

To choose a wall color for your room, pull a neutral color from the pattern of the rug or draperies. This color will then determine the basic hue from which wall colors for other rooms in the home will be determined.

Analyzing the Room for Furniture Placement

On observation of a room, analyze the placement of furnishings. Make a rough sketch of each room, locating windows, doors, and all other items according to what you have learned in Unit I in "Drawing A Rough Sketch." Exact measurements will not be necessary. By this time in your studies, you will have developed enough of an understanding of proper furniture placement that you will be able to visually assess the space for placement.

Note the largest furniture pieces in the room. In the Living Room this is the sofa, piano, bookcase, or entertainment center. Using your knowledge of principles regarding focal point and balance, sketch into your rough sketch where these items are best to be located.

The Uncluttered Look

The look you are going for in a staging is an uncluttered look, however, not to the point where a welcoming atmosphere is sacrificed. Providing both a clean, uncluttered feel and maintaining a "welcome home" mood requires making right choices in what is left in the room after purging.

Review your UNIT I lesson entitled "FURNITURE LAYOUT. Refer to the following ROOM BALANCE diagram inserted on the following pages. Observe the process of furniture placement from **Fig. 8** through to **Fig. 14**. Notice that the largest and most functional items are placed first, then furnishings filling secondary functions. Observe the placement of large furniture on the axis of the room, and how seating arrangements are placed in a "Conversation Grouping" around a natural or created focal point. Keeping these rules in mind, determine the placement of furnishings in your re-design of each room.

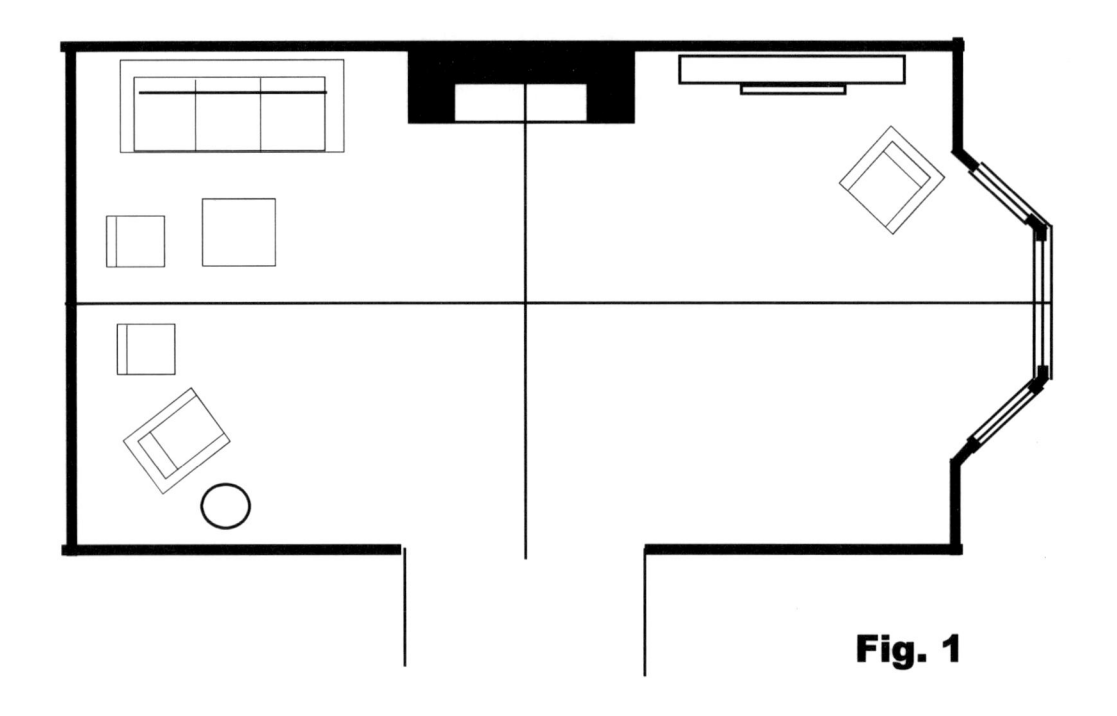

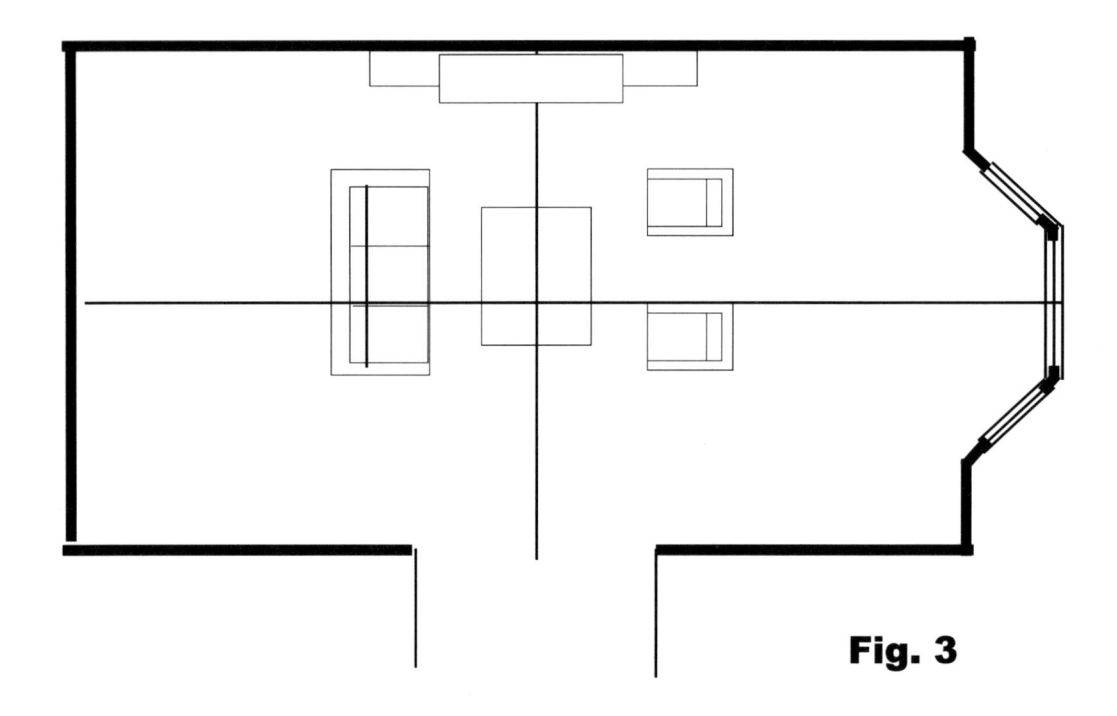

Fig. 1

Fig. 3

Fig. 2

Fig. 4

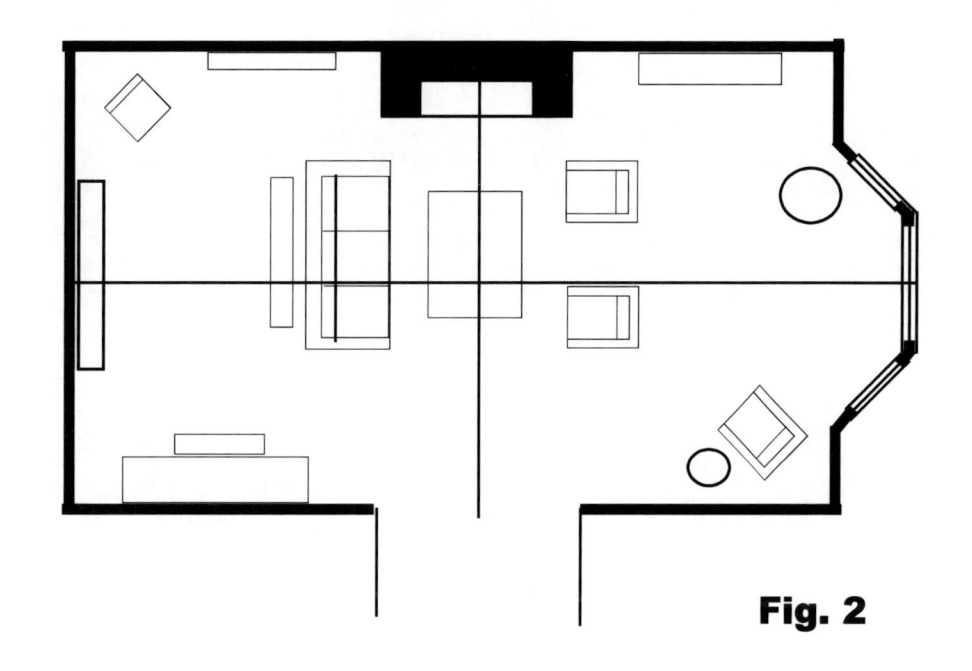

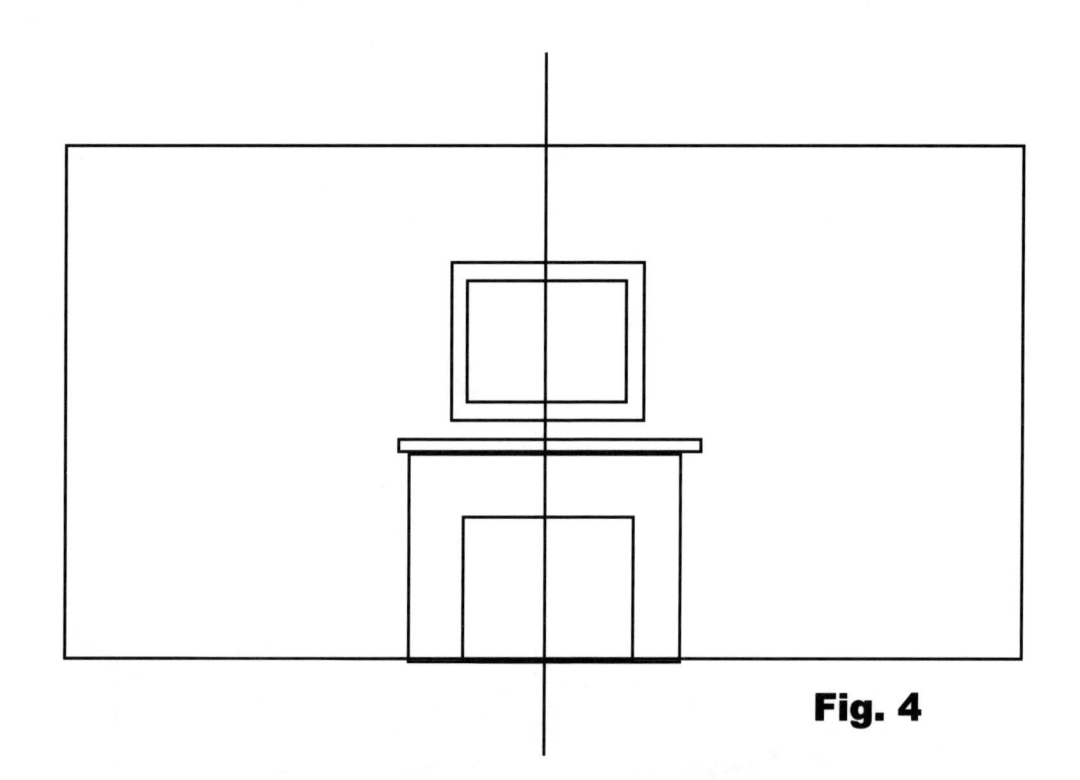

ROOM BALANCE A

Interior Design For Today

171

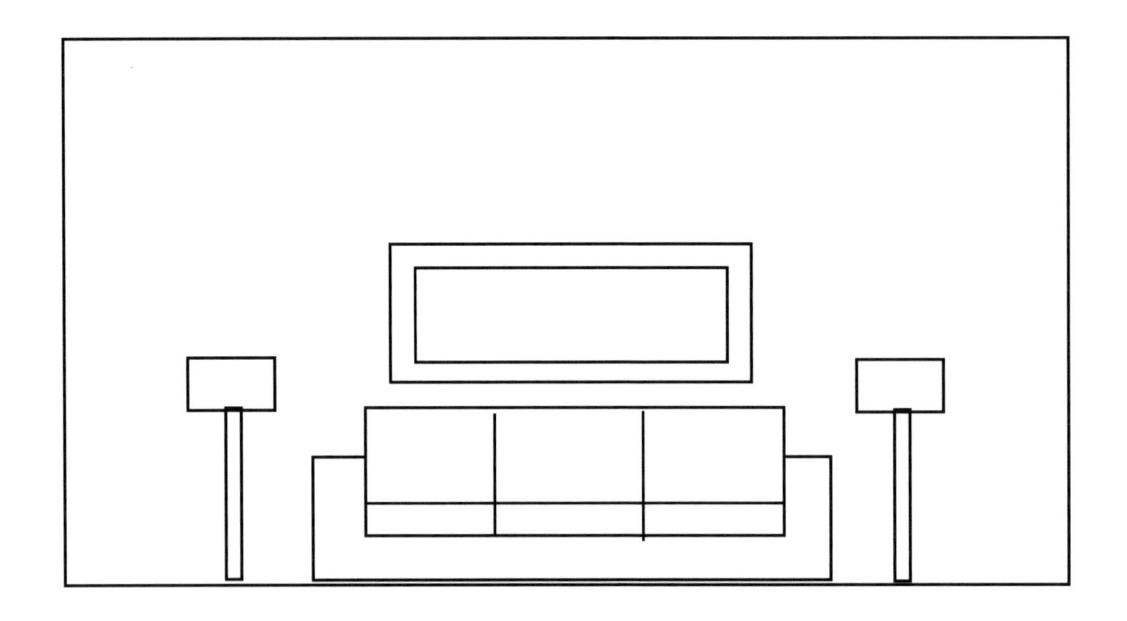

Fig. 5

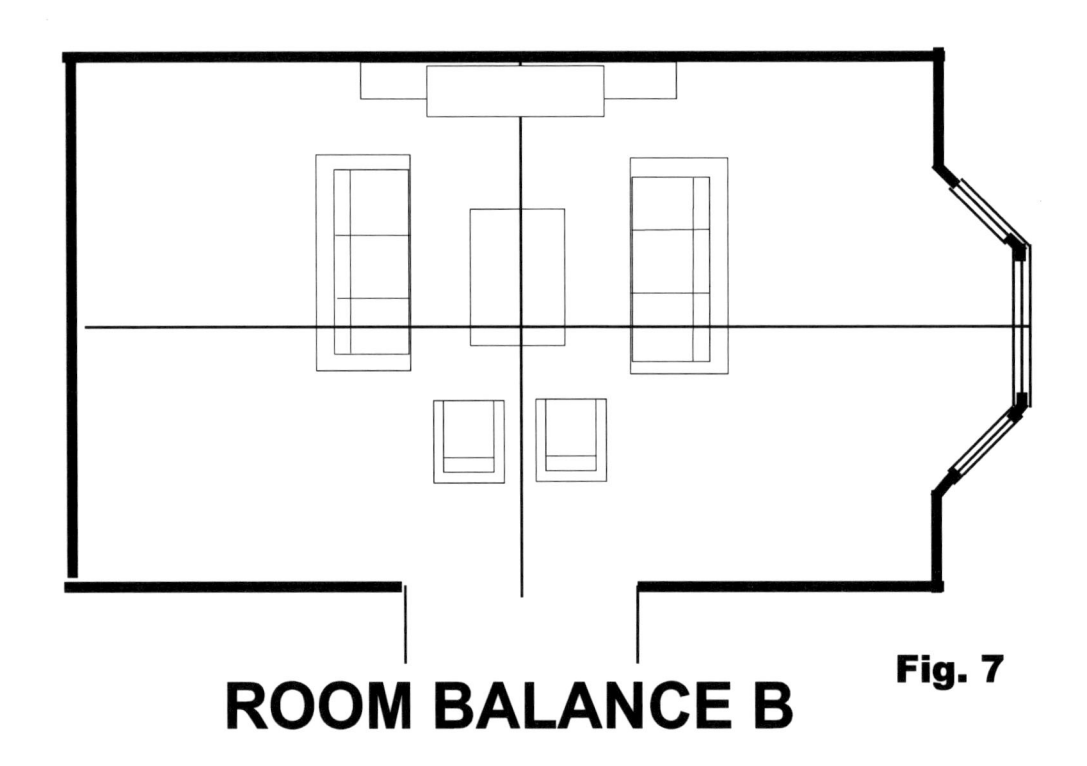

ROOM BALANCE B **Fig. 7**

Fig. 6

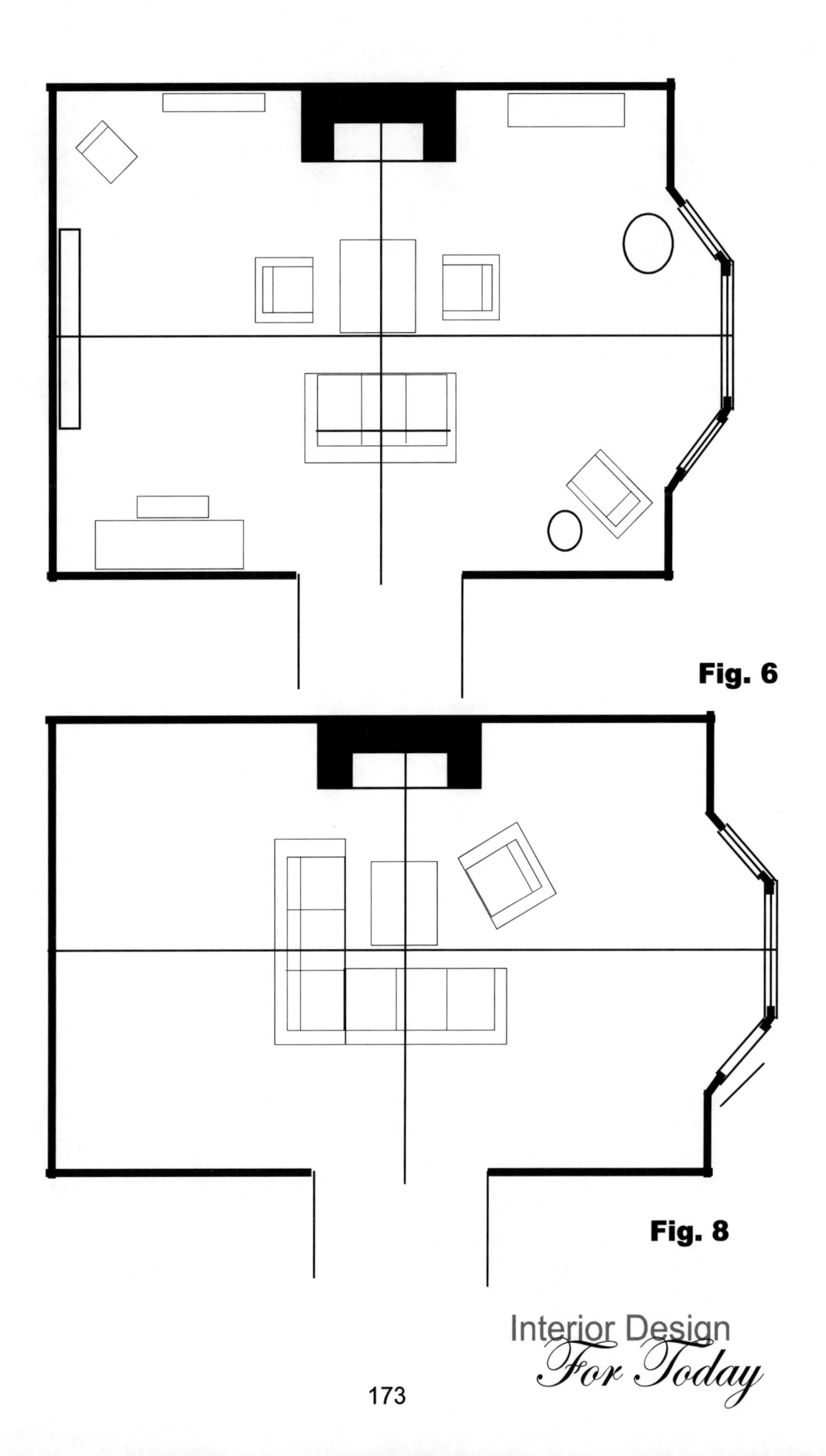

Fig. 8

Interior Design
For Today

173

Fig. 9

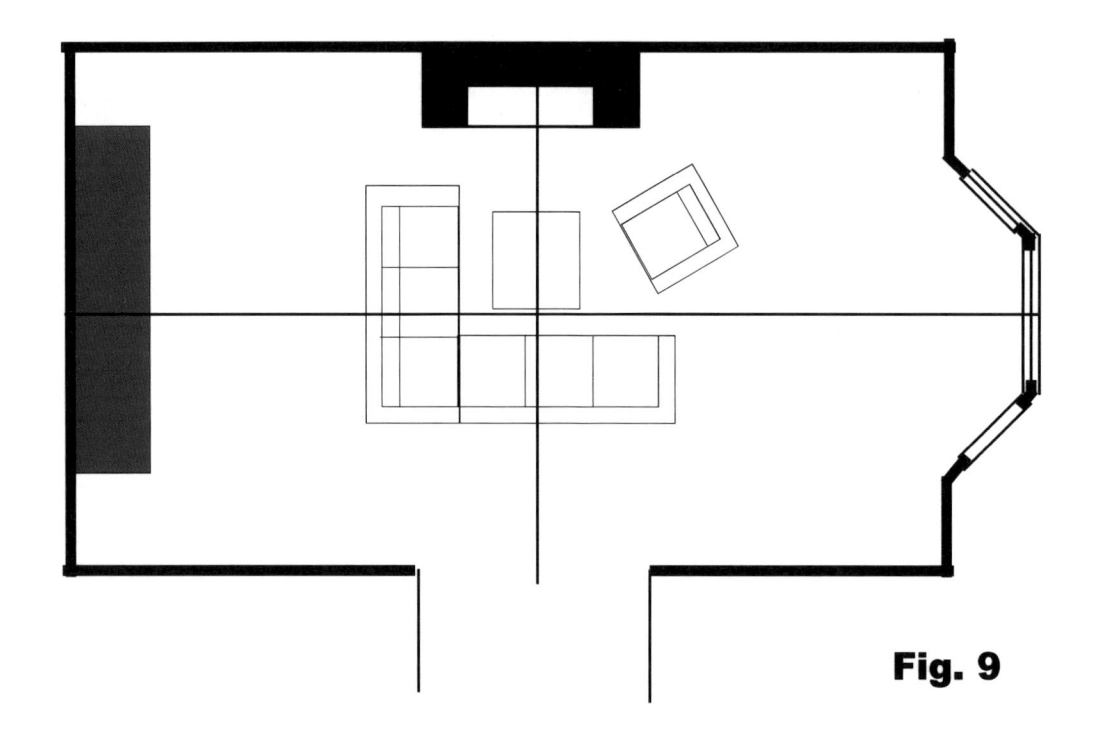

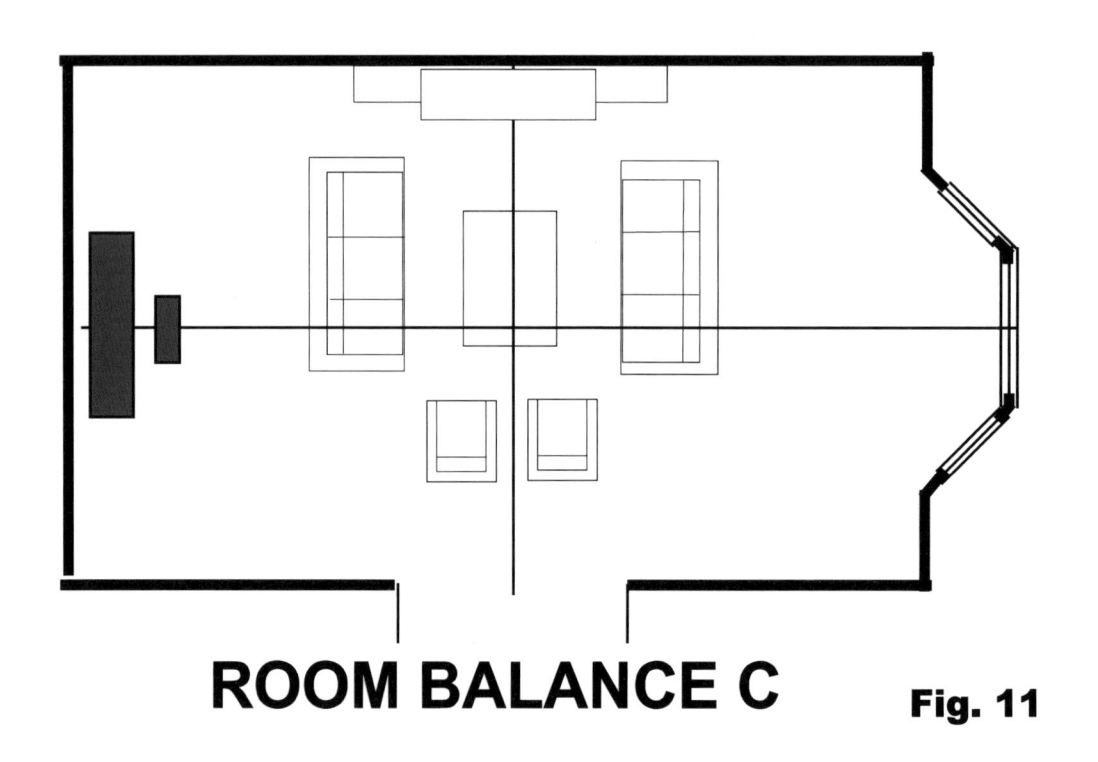

ROOM BALANCE C   **Fig. 11**

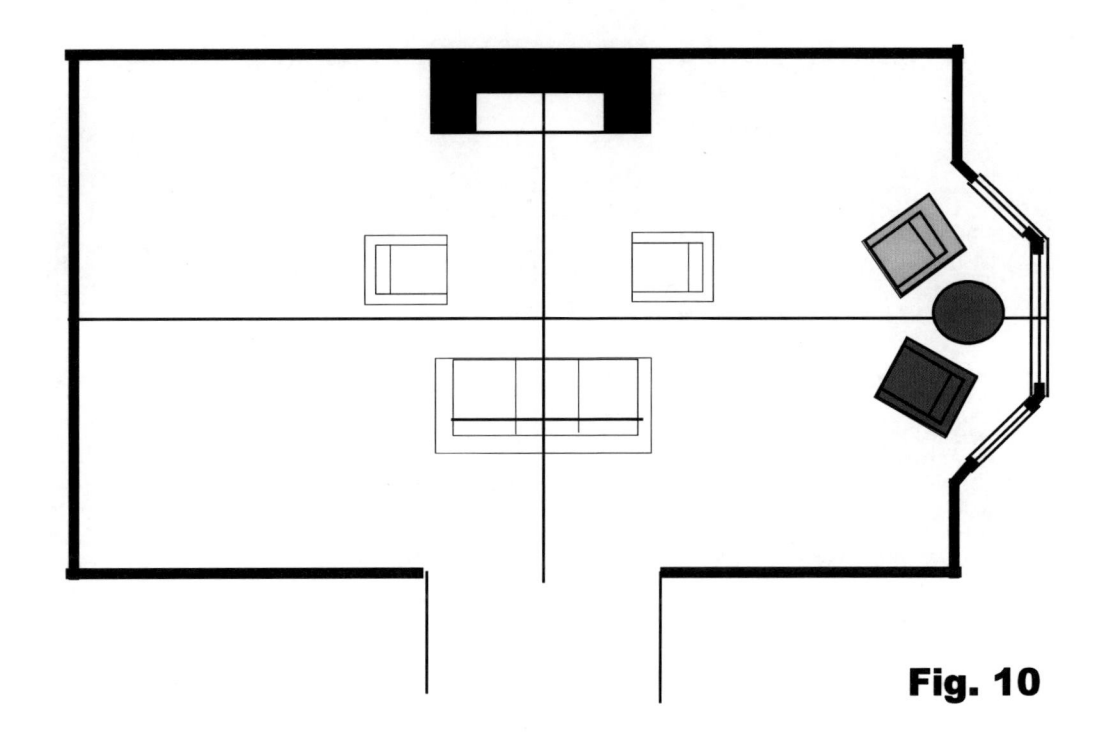

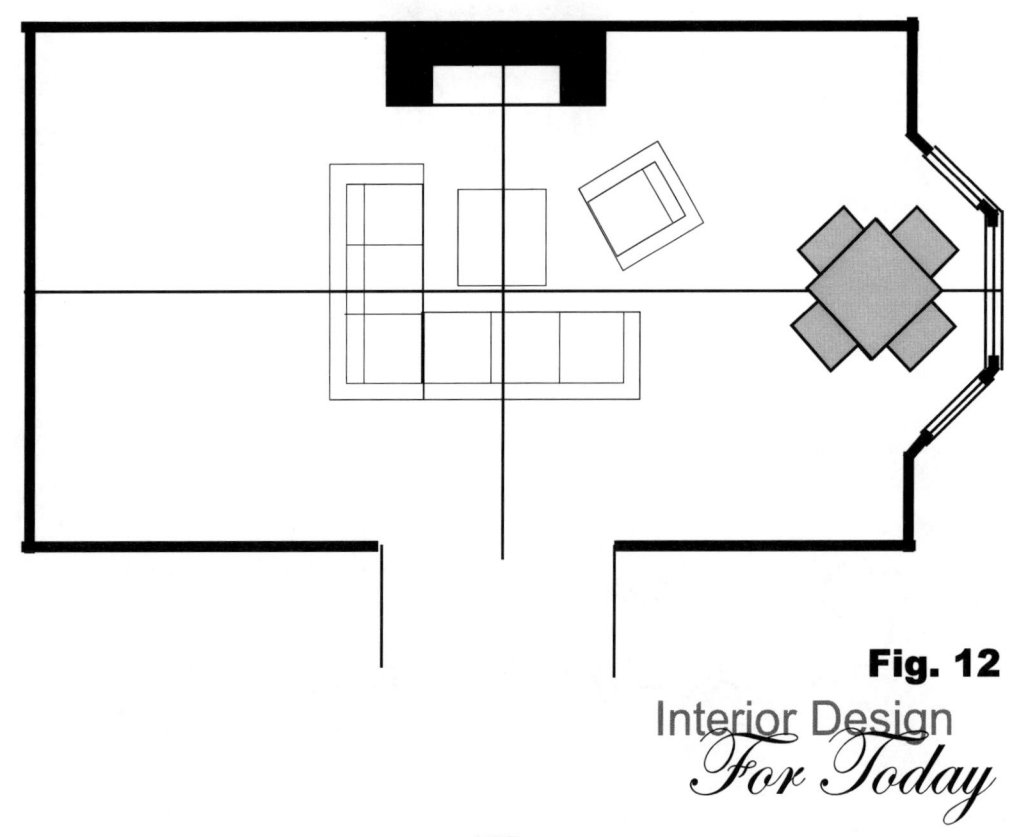

Fig. 10

Fig. 12
Interior Design
For Today

Fig. 13

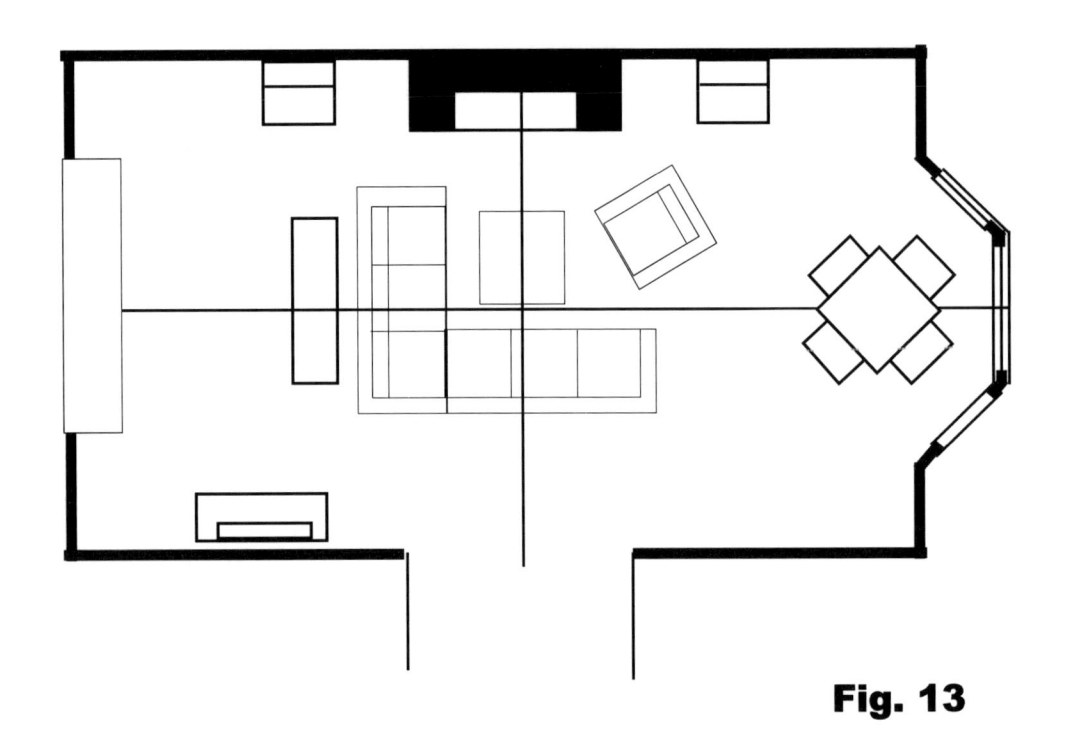

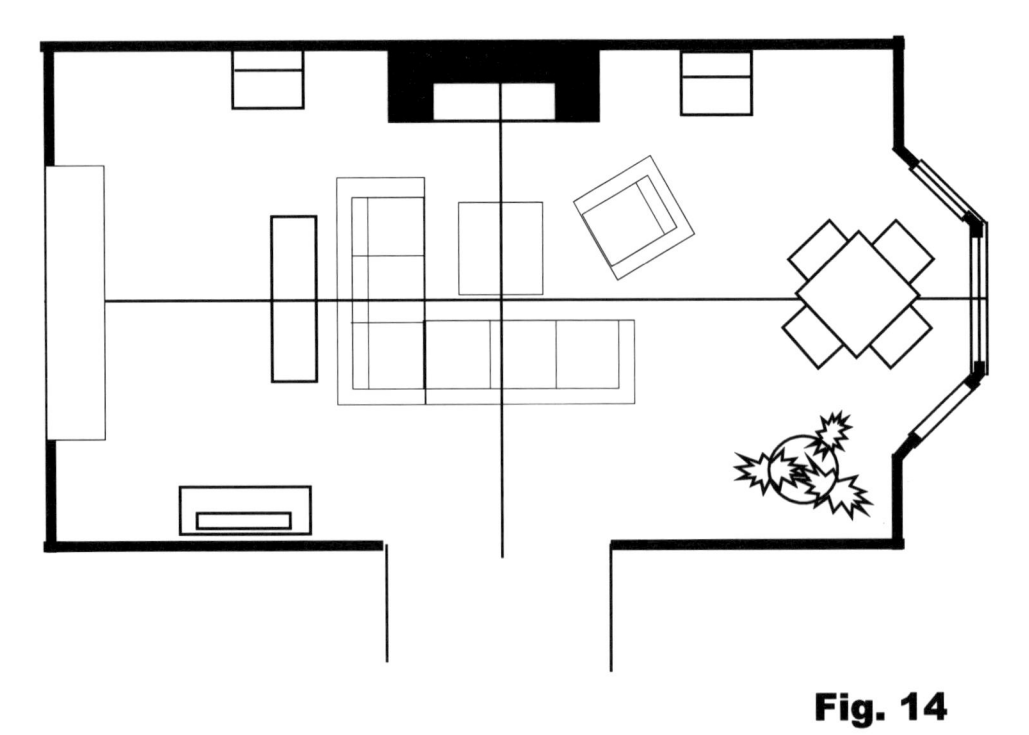

Fig. 14

ROOM BALANCE D

Scale & Symmetry

Next, apply the rules of scale and symmetry to your placement of furnishings. Use your client's most suitable artwork or picture groups to advantage, placing them for maximum impact.

Unity in Style

Unfortunately, unless a homeowner has made an effort to co-ordinate the style of furnishing throughout the home, unifying a space may be a challenge. However, harmony can be achieved through various other methods not limited by style. For instance, the shape of a piece of furniture will determine how it "fits" the space.

Pay special attention to the line of a piece of furniture. Is it simple, or ornate? Grouping the ornate with the simple will present confusion rather than harmony, therefore, keep these separate if possible, and remove those pieces that just don't fit. Less is more, and the purged piece will not be missed. Instead, fill a gaping space with a large plant that is neutral in its dictates.

Using Color to Unify

To bring harmony throughout a home, use a color repeatedly throughout. As you have already learned, a color palette consists of two or three co-ordinating colors. Use these in small amounts from room to room. Pick up the orange, for example, from the Living Room carpet, repeat it in a throw or throw pillows, then extend it to the kitchen in dishware, and in a darker shade, to tableware in the Dining Room. Use the blue hue of favorite Bedroom draperies with its more mellow hue in co-ordinating blue shams and bedding, as well as in bath towels for the ensuite bathroom. Take the yellow from a favorite painting and reintroduce it in a bouquet of fresh-cut daffodils for the kitchen table. Against a neutral backdrop of fluent wall color running from room to room throughout the home, these shots of color will not overwhelm, but instead prove to add a welcome touch of warmth while bringing harmony from one room to the next.

Updates to Furnishings

When re-designing a room, the opportunity exists to take advantage of furnishings that are already in use rather than to import new. However, though a piece of furniture may be structurally sound, its color may clash with other pieces around it, or its finish might be stained or chipped. Or it might lack definition, character, and style. Applying paint and new hardware to give it a neutral, more sophisticated look, can transform a boring piece of furniture into a feature that enhances the style and harmony in a room. For instance, applying a coat of black paint and polished chrome hardware to an old pair of end tables or bed-side tables add sophistication while blending in with any style. Paint a wooden dining table and chairs gloss white to freshen its look and add sparkle.

Add the New

New color-co-ordinating bedding for a tired-looking bed, a new fitted cover for a clashing sofa, new upholstery for worn dining chairs, a new rug or throw pillows, and a new color-co-ordinated set of dishware to be put on display, can all add to an updated look.

Kitchen Updates

Depending on the scope of the re-design, upgrades to the kitchen will vary. If not limited by time, as with a staging, the re-design of a kitchen might include re-faced cabinetry. However, if time is an issue, a coat of paint in a neutral hue (white is a good choice) will do wonders to freshen up existing cabinetry. Consider new, updated hardware, as well as a new stylish faucet.

The kitchen is a good place to aim for a clean, streamlined, uncluttered space. Brighten it up with updated "white light" halogen fixtures where possible, and consider clean-lined roller shades on windows to replace dowdy fabric curtains.

Updating a Bathroom

On a low budget and shortage of time, the bathroom benefits most from a fresh coat of paint, updated faucets, lighting fixtures, and hardware, and a new shower curtain. Add finishing touches with towels and accessories strategically placed for most impact.

Fix What Needs Fixing

It goes without saying, that it is important to have all elements of a kitchen and bathroom in good repair. If a tap drips, have it fixed. If a door knob is loose, have it fitted properly. If hinges droop, replace them. These final touches all contribute to a successful re-design and impressive presentation of a well cared-for home.

The Interior Design Presentation

Up to this point you have studied all the ins and outs of interior design. You have drawn up floorplans, furniture layouts, lighting plans, studied and prepared *Furniture Style Worksheets* for your rooms. You have studied color and learned to apply it to a *Color Scheme* for each of you rooms in the form of fabrics and paint colors. You have become equipped with practical knowledge in design. In this lesson you will learn how to prepare and present your **Interior Design Package** to a client who has commissioned you for an Interior Design job. This package will include **Presentation Boards** and the method you have chosen of **Charging Out Your Services**.

Preparing Presentation Boards

The Presentation

Once you have agreed to take on an Interior Design project for a client, you will prepare presentation boards that display your package.

This presentation will include a floorplan with a furniture and lighting layout for each room, fabric and paint color samples, furniture and lighting style samples, window and bed treatment displays, built-in displays, as well as a budget for the job.

At this point, your client may veto some of your choices and you will have to reassess them and re-present new choices. The budget will be discussed, and agreed upon before work can begin.

Floorplan Presentation Board

You have already prepared a floorplan with a furniture layout as well as a lighting plan. Your presentation board is a combination of the two. Refer to the DINING ROOM FLOORPLAN PRESENTATION BOARD for help. The Floorplan is presented horizontally and centered on a decorative board and labeled.

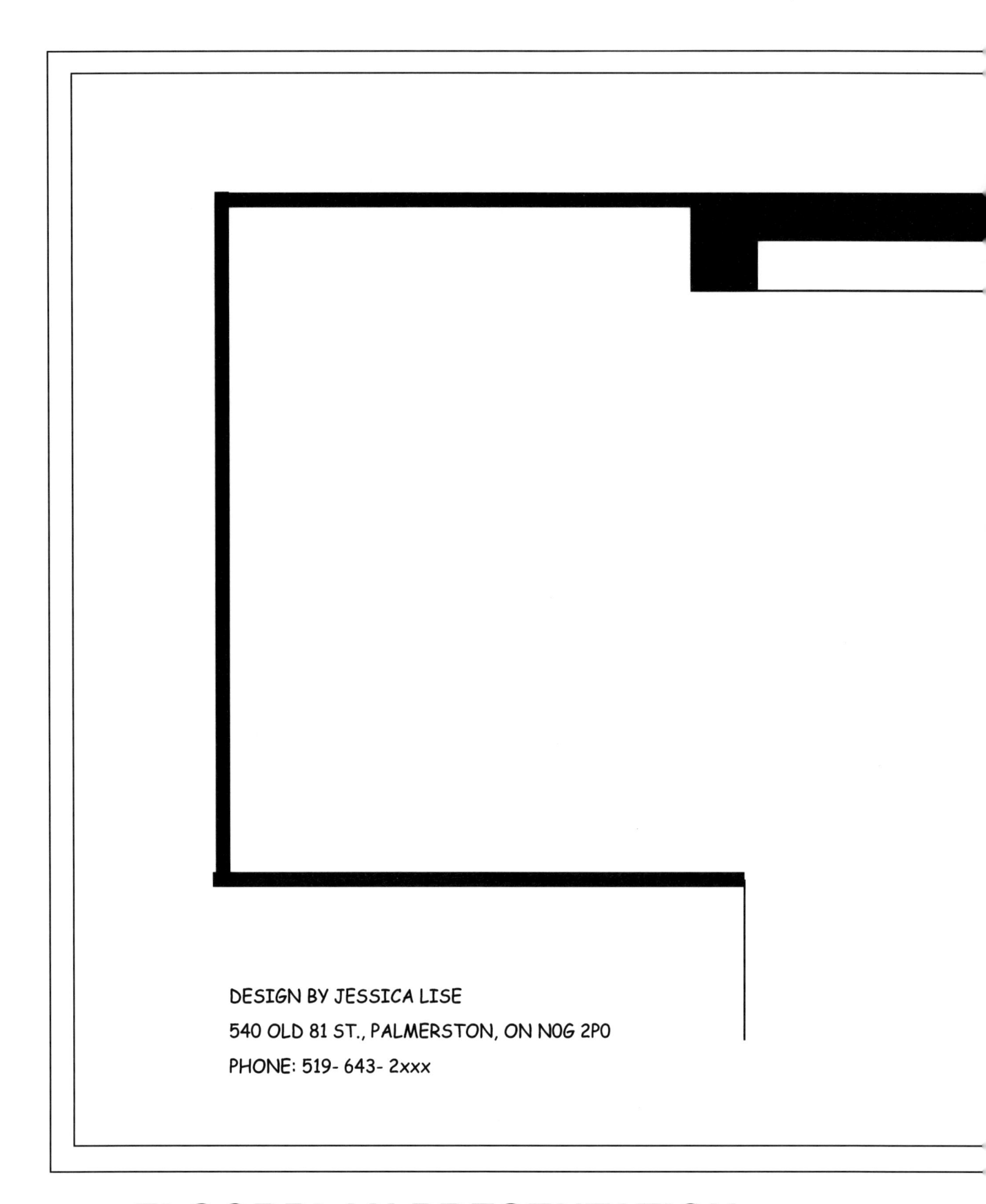

DESIGN BY JESSICA LISE
540 OLD 81 ST., PALMERSTON, ON N0G 2P0
PHONE: 519- 643- 2xxx

FLOORPLAN PRESENTATION

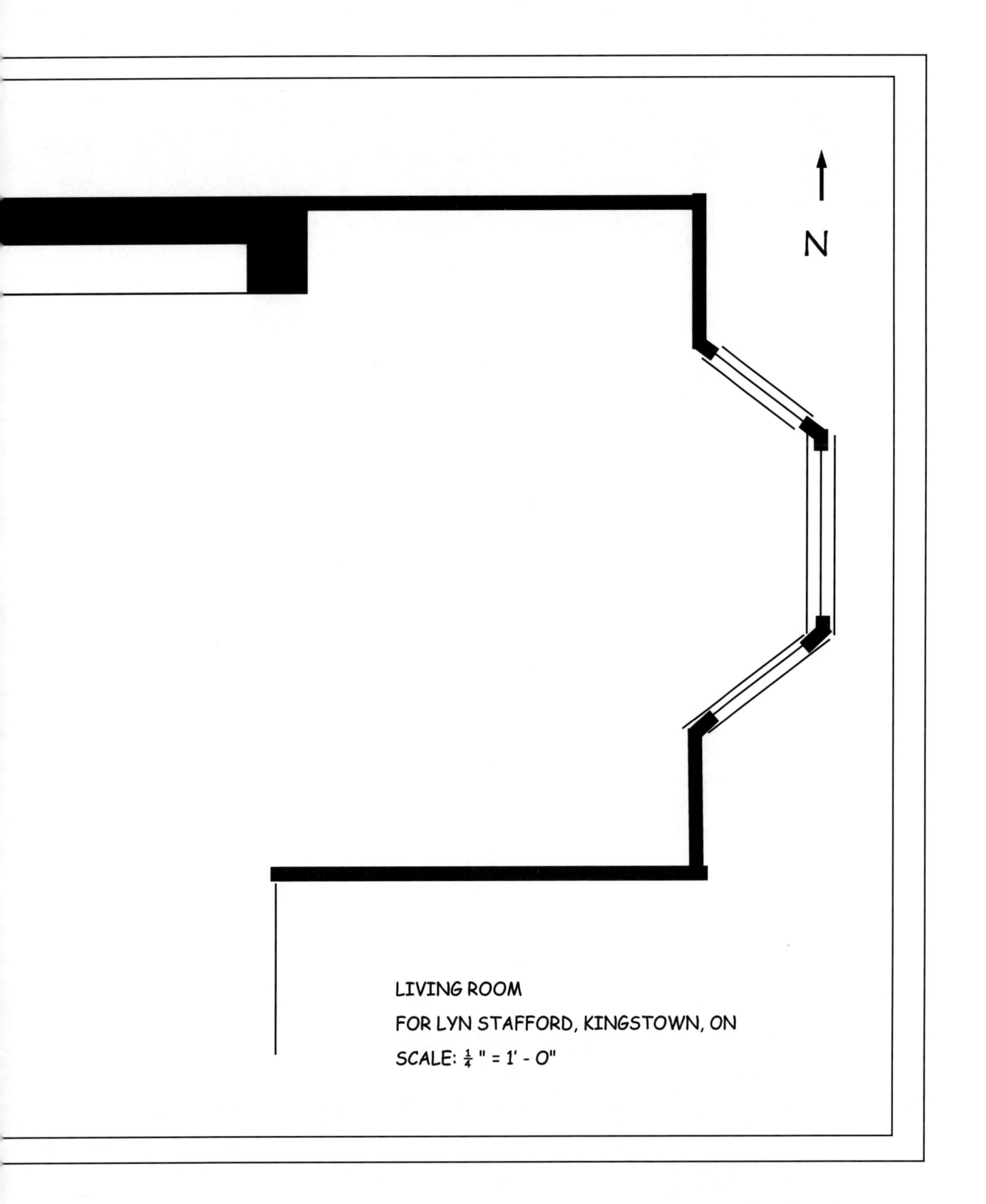

LIVING ROOM
FOR LYN STAFFORD, KINGSTOWN, ON
SCALE: ¼ " = 1' - 0"

Color Scheme Presentation Board

The next board to be prepared is the Color Scheme Board. Fabric and paint samples will be mounted and neatly displayed on a decorative labeled board. Refer to the COLOR SCHEME PRESENTATION BOARD for help.

Furniture Presentation Board

The next board to be prepared is the Furniture Presentation Board. Refer to the DINING ROOM FURNITURE PRESENTATION BOARD and LIVING ROOM FURNITURE PRESENTATION BOARDs for help. Drawings or pictures of furnishings to be used in the design project are mounted onto a decorative labeled board.

Window Treatment Presentation Board

A next board to prepare is one which features the window treatment you have planned to use for each window in the room. Drawings or pictures to illustrate style of draperies and hardware chosen are mounted onto a decorative labeled board with as much detail as possible. Drapery fabric samples are added to this display. Refer to the BEDROOM WINDOW TREATMENT PRESENTATION and the BAY WINDOW TREATMENT PRESENTATION for help.

Bed Treatment Board

If your Interior Design project includes a bedroom design, you will present a Bed Treatment Presentation Board that features the bed treatment you have planned for this room. It will include fabric samples. Refer to the BED TREATMENT PRESENTATION for help.

Budget Presentation

The Budget Presentation is not mounted on a decorative board, but instead is typed up neatly on 8½" x 11" letterhead with each individual item numbered in correspondence with furnishings on your floorplan. The budget includes the cost of all material purchases plus your commission on these purchases, as well as the cost of all service contracts with trades people. Because service costs will be estimated for the job, it is presented as an estimate. Refer to the BUDGET PRESENTATION for help.

RICHARDSON DINING ROOM

COLOR SCHEME PRESENTATION

COLOR SCHEME

Interior Design
For Today

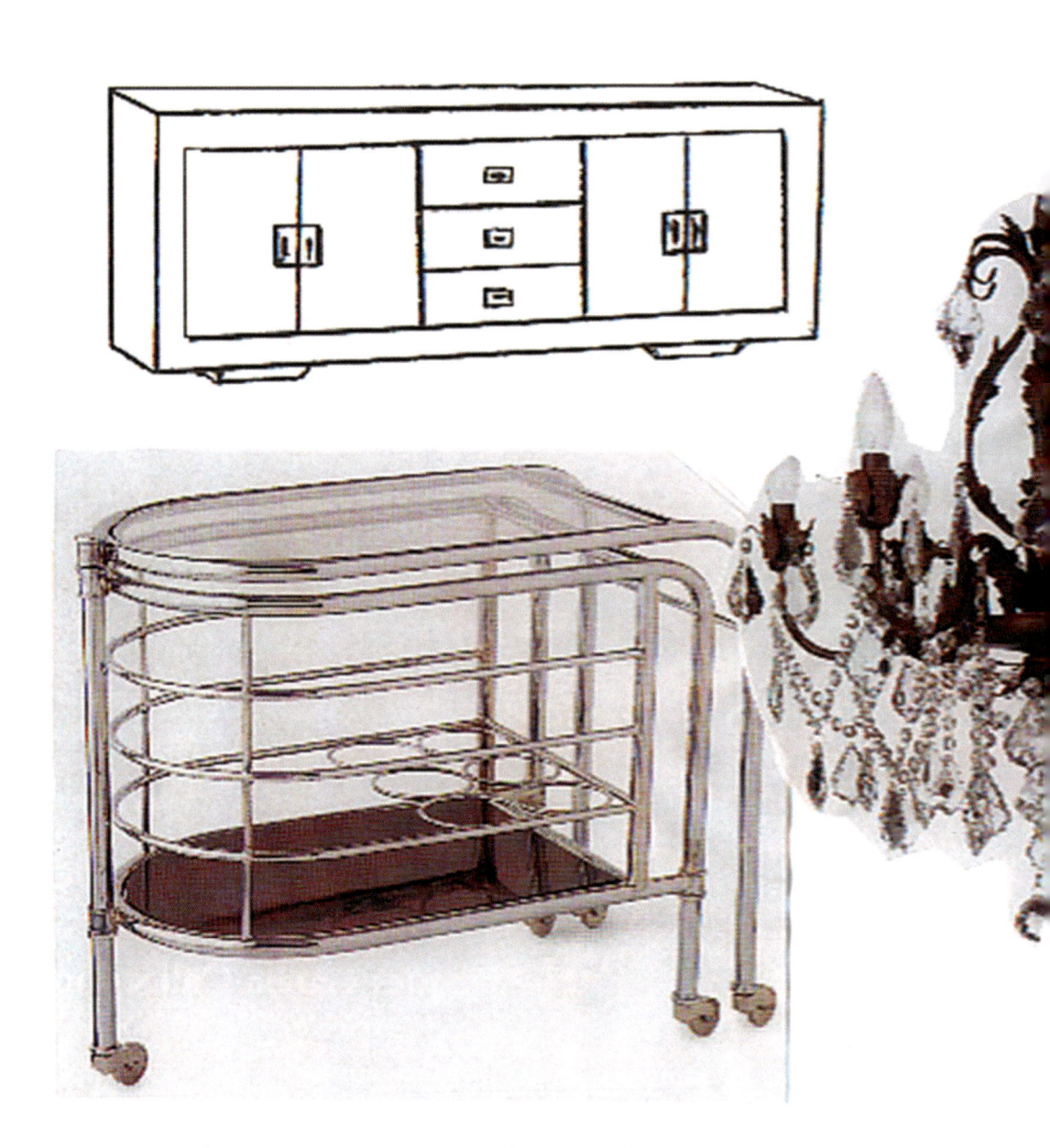

RICHARDSON DINING ROOM

DINING ROOM FURNITURE

FURNITURE

Interior Design For Today

Living Room

LIVING ROOM FURNITURE

Furniture

Interior Design
For Today

4"
wooden Board
Traverse Rod
Angle iron
Face of valance

B

C

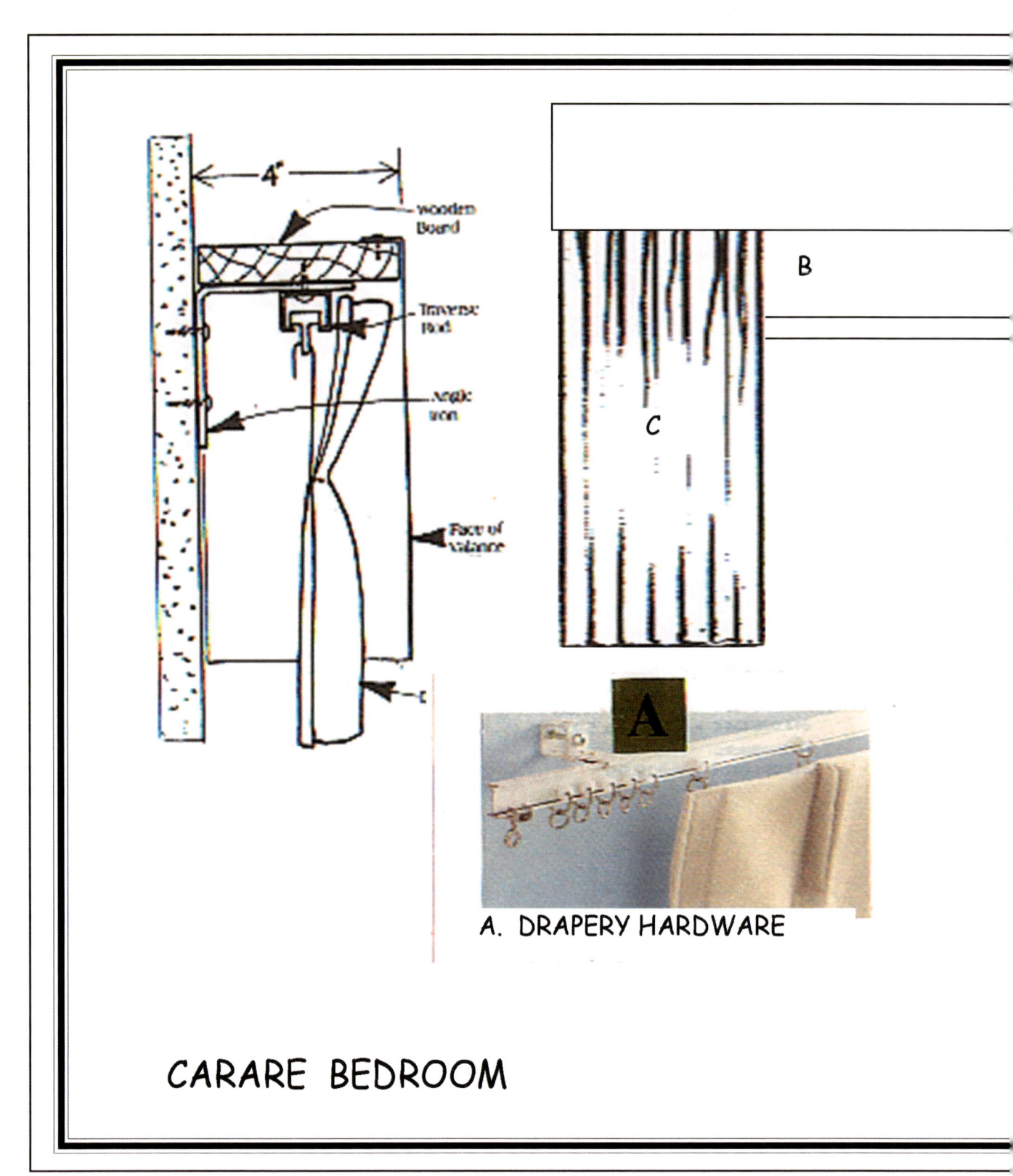

A

A. DRAPERY HARDWARE

CARARE BEDROOM

BEDROOM WINDOW TREATMENT

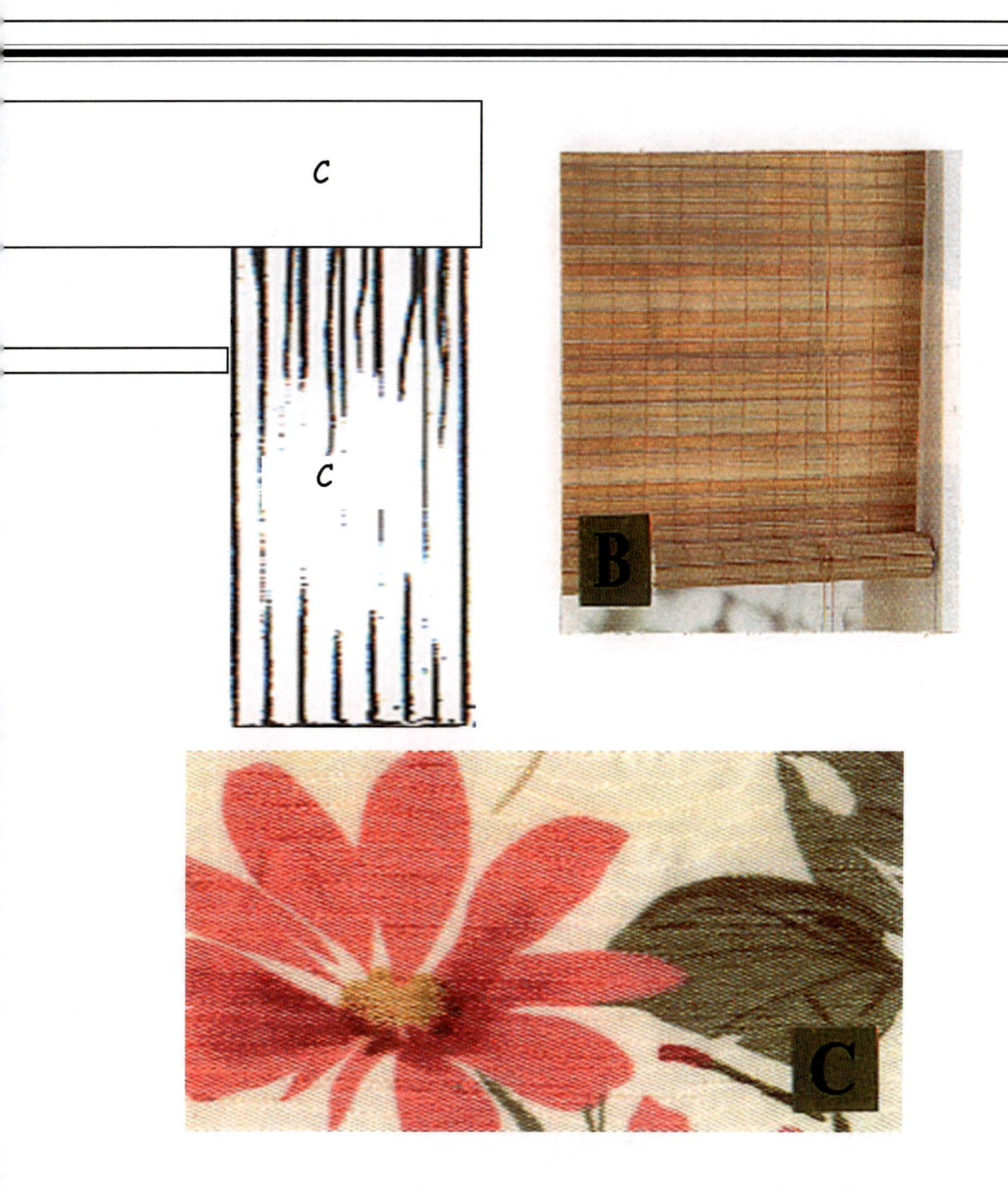

C

C

B

C

WINDOW TREATMENT

© Copyright 2013

Interior Design
For Today

RICHARDSON DINING ROOM

BAY WINDOW TREATMENT

© Copyright 2013

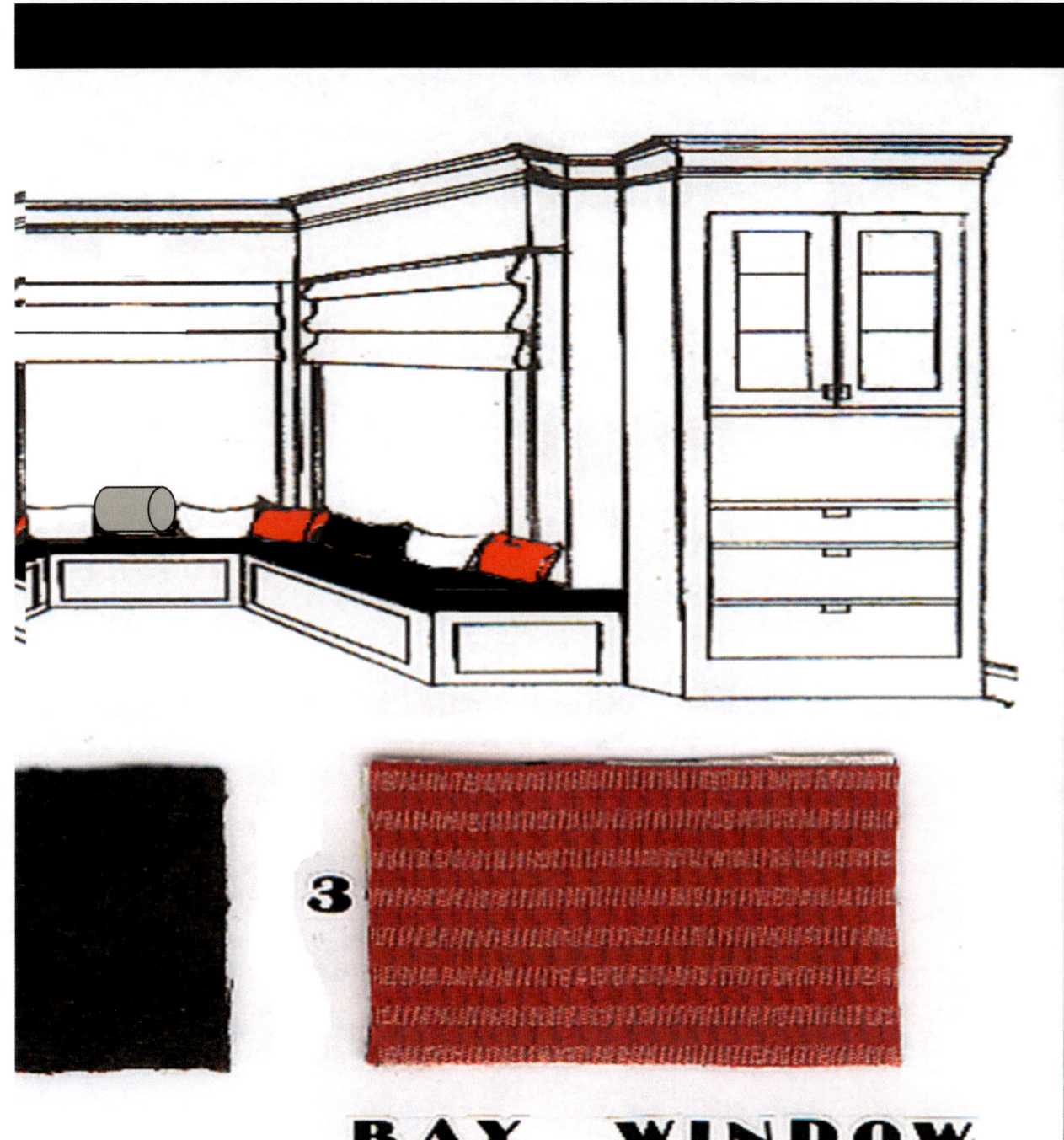

BAY WINDOW TREATMENT

Interior Design For Today

BED TREATMENT

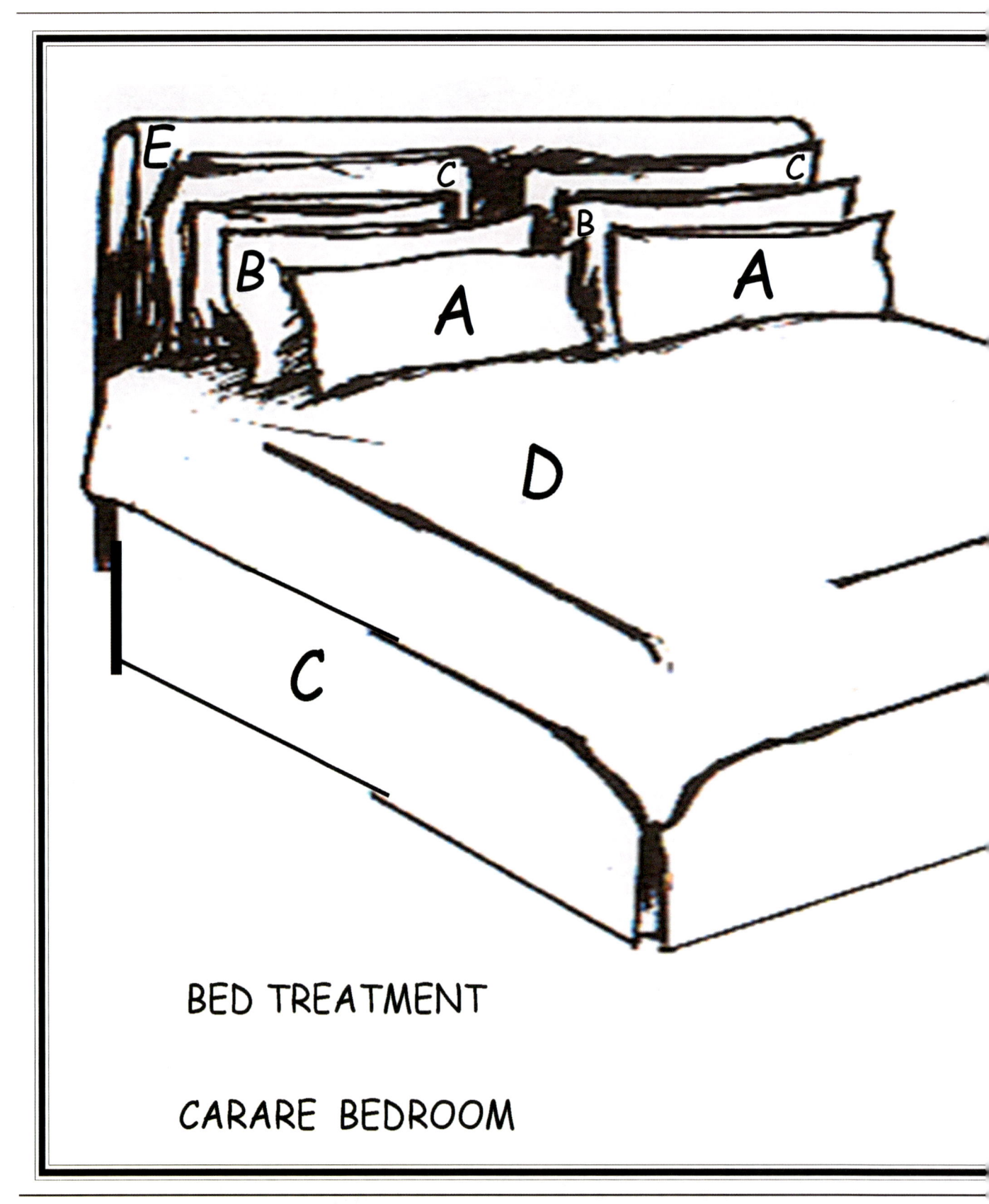

CARARE BEDROOM

BED TREATMENT PRESENTATION

197

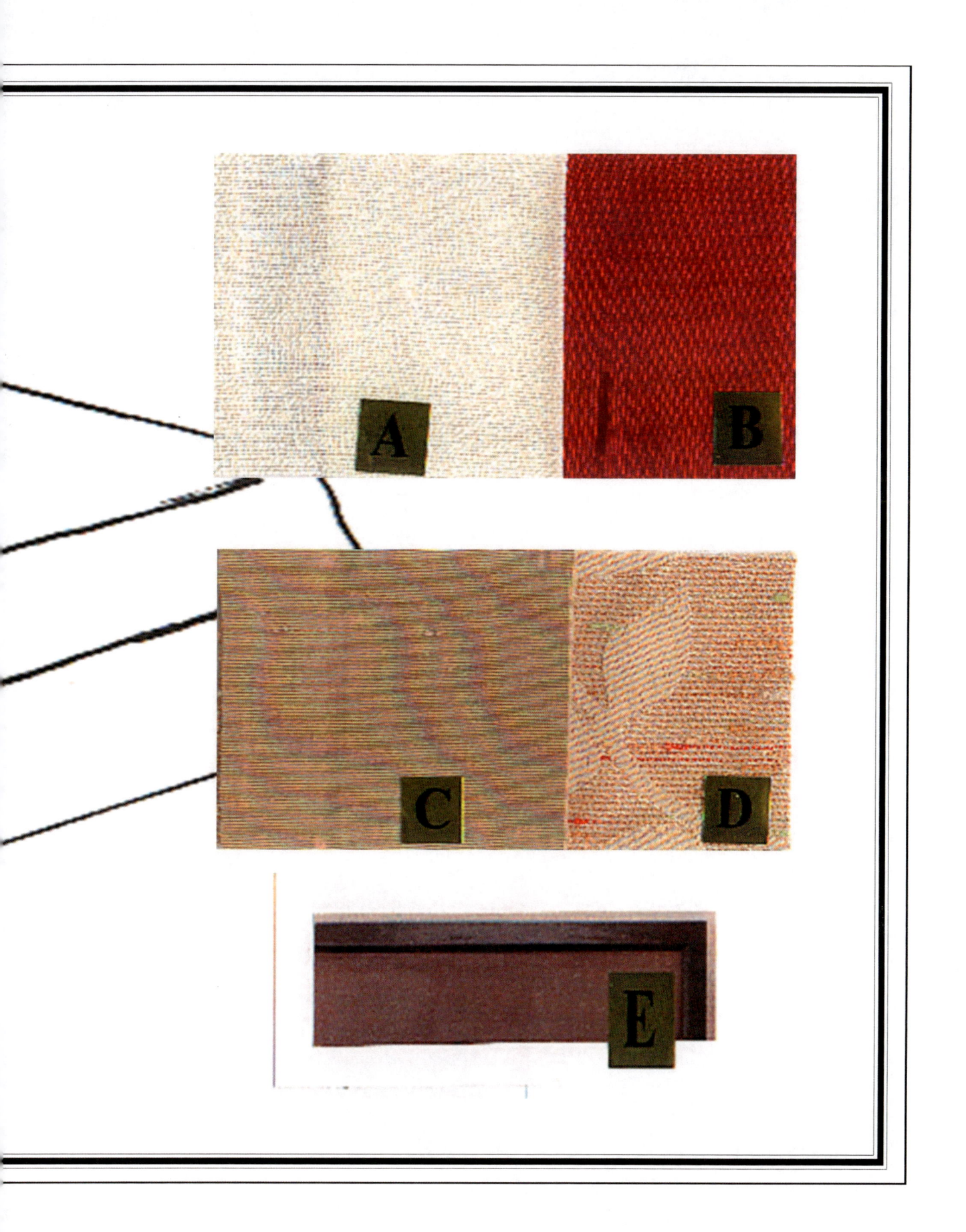

INSTYLE DECOR

Interior Design & Decorating

222 Durham St., Stratford, ON N2A 1Z7

December 8, 2007

Mr. & Mrs. Richardson, 218 Maple Cresent, Teviotdale, ON

1. Dining Table	$2100.00
2. Dining Chairs x 8 @ $398.00 each	3184.00
3. Buffet	2850.00
4. Mirror	549.00
5. Picture	349.98
6. Wine Cart	349.97
7. Chandelier	1345.00
8. Buffet Lamps x 2 @149.98 each	299.96
9. Wiring for and installation of striplights, cabinet lighting, recessed down lights and mounting of chandelier - 5 hours @ $45.00 per hr. (includes electrical wire and switches)	225.00
- 3, 34.5" Aluminum Fluoro Bar System strip lights @ $66.57 per bar	199.71
- 4, 4" potlight housing kts with tilting white bimble trim and flood lamps @ $30.07 each	120.28
10. Installation of Crown Moulding and changing out of baseboard	
- 4 hours @ $35.00 per hr.	140.00
- 2 pieces 14', 1 piece 16', 1 piece 12' "Ogee" Crown Moulding, 56 linear ft. @ $3.00 per linear ft.	168.00
- 1 piece 16', 1 piece 12', 1 piece 10' ,6" wide "French" baseboard, 38 linear ft. @ $1.73 per linear ft.	65.74
11. Paint out ceiling, walls, and trim	
- 10 hours @ $25.00 per hour	250.00
- 2 gal. tinted latex primer @ 27.99 per gal.	55.98
- 3 gal. eggshell Dark Color Accent @ $51.99 per gal.	155.97
- 1 gal. semi-gloss alkyd paint @ 36.99 per gal.	36.99

12. Refinishing of Floor

   - Supplies and Labour   1600.00

13. Built-ins around Bay Window

   - estimated cost of material and labour   3000.00

14. Fabrication of window seat cushions and pillows

   - 3 cushions @ $80.00 per cushion, 11 pillows @$55.00 per cushion (includes pillow forms)   845.00

   - 3, 3" thick foam pieces 48" x 22" for window seats, @38.40 per piece   115.20

   - 4 m. Heavy Jacquard 60% Viscose/40% Polyester @ $21.98 per m.   87.92

   - 1.4 m. Colorado Decor 64% Polyester/36% Rayon @ $14.98 per m.   20.98

   - 1.4 m. Romance Moire 100% Polyester @ $18.98 per m.   26.57

   - 1 m. Natural Jacquard @14.98 per m.   14.98

15. Fabrication and Installation of Roman Blinds and Valance

   - 3 x 4' x 6' Roman Blinds at $20.00 per sq. ft.   1440.00

   - 8.8 m "Flanders" White/Black Newport Sateen Collection, 52% Cotton/48% Rayon @ $19.98 per m.   175.82

   - 8.8 m cotton lining @ $3.75 per m.   33.00

   - Valance   180.00

   - 1.85 m. "Flanders" White/Black Newport Sateen Collection @ $19.98/m.   36.96

   - 1.85 m.. cotton lining @ $3.75 per m.   6.94

BUDGET PRESENTATION

Interior Design For Today

Charging out your Services

"Selling" Your Services

Prior to preparing your presentation package for your client, an agreement to contract the work project needs to be made between you, the Interior Designer, and your client, therefore, a plan needs to be in place to charge out your services.

At first meeting with a potential client, you will make yourself available to meet at his/her home. As you have learned earlier on in your studies, you will bring along your "ICE BREAKER" questionnaire to gather information about your potential client's preferences and scope of the work intended. At this meeting, you will have opportunity to "sell" your services, therefore you will need to present your package as an Interior Designer. You will need to decide how you will present your services and at what cost to your client. Have a pamphlet prepared in advance with this information readily available.

Letters of Agreement

If a second meeting is arranged as a guarantee that you have been given the project, this meeting will solicit a signed agreement between you and your client. A fee for your time is also appropriate. This fee is referred to as a *Flat Fee,* that you can charge out at this meeting upon the signing of a **Letter of Agreement**.

A second fee you might charge out to your client, is that of a *Room Design Fee*. This fee may be divided into two separate installments, 50% to be charged out prior to your assessment of the room and rough sketch, and the rest to be charged out prior to the presentation of your design plan, thus guaranteeing that the hours you spend drawing floor and furniture plans, scouting for fabric and paint colors, and preparing a presentation, will not go un-rewarded. Of course, your pamphlet will well describe these charges in advance so that there will be agreement regarding them.

When the design presentation with budget has been made and agreed upon, and a room plan worksheet with written details of the work has been presented, another Letter of Agreement might be signed to guarantee that you, indeed, have the contract, and can proceed with the work schedule. Refer to the LETTER OF AGREEMENT for help. This Letter of Agreement will present, in full, your method of charging out the planning, purchasing, and supervision of work regarding the project.

Apart from charging a Flat and Design Fee, other income gained in the overseeing of the design project may include a commission on all your purchases and on labor services, as well as charging out your time at the work site at an hourly rate. This is just one income option as an Interior Designer.

Charge Out Options

There are various other optional methods to the one above of charging out your services. One is to waive the flat and design fees and charge yourself out at an hourly rate as well as collect commission on all planning, purchasing, and supervision of the work. Billing out-of-pocket job related expenses back to the client is part of this method.

Another option is to take sole compensation for all planning, purchasing and supervision of work in a lump sum to be charged out in installments as the work progresses.

Still other options include a sole charge by hourly rate, sole commission on purchases and services, or a combination of design fees, drafting fees, hourly rate, and commission on planning, purchasing, and supervision.

Whatever choice you make in how you charge out your services, draft up your Letter of Agreement in a clear, precise form so that there is no misunderstanding or misinterpretation of costs involved for your client. This will bolster a good working relationship and guarantee success from beginning to end on the project.

SAMPLE LETTER OF AGREEMENT

Date:

(Client's Name)(Client's Address)

Dear:

This letter will confirm our method of operation in connection with the work to be done relative to your residence at the above address.

Fifty percent of a Flat Fee of $150.00 (plus applicable sales tax) and 50% of an additional Room Design Fee of $150.00 per room (plus applicable sales tax) will have been paid by you prior to the signing of this agreement.

This agreement includes an assessment of the work that needs to be done by observing and filling out questionnaires regarding the space. Discussion will take place to pin point style and mood to be attained through the design process. Furnishings, carpeting, draperies, etc. to be kept in the design will be noted and a rough budget will be proposed. In preparation for the Design Plan Presentation, working photos, measurements, and rough sketches of the room and furnishings will be taken.

At a future date, outstanding Flat + Room Design Fees will be charged to you, and a **Presentation of the Design Plan** will be made. This presentation includes a Floor Plan with Furniture & Lighting Layout, Color Scheme Board, Furniture & Lighting Samples, Window Treatment Plan, Bed Treatment Plan (if applicable), including fabric Samples. A Room Planning Worksheet, with written details of the work, and a budget for this work will also be presented. Discussion of the plan, noting any minor changes, will follow, and a decision to proceed with the work will be confirmed with the signing of an **Agreement to Proceed**.

Payment made prior to the signing of this **Agreement to Design** and a future payment made prior to a following **Agreement to**

Proceed will cover all design fees.

Other future costs to you will include the following:

1. Cost of purchases + 25% Commission on all purchases, including paint and paint supplies, flooring, carpeting, furniture, lighting fixtures, rugs, draperies, accessories, hardware, fabrics, sewing supplies and notions, etc.

2. Cost of contracted work of trades people + 25% Commission on all work done by trades people, including electrical, plumbing, carpentry, upholstering, outside fabrication of draperies, pillows, bedding, etc.

3. $20.00 per hour to prep and paint walls and furniture

4. Fabrication of draperies, blinds, pillows, bedding @ $20.00 per hour

5. Assistance with general labour on site @ $25.00 per hour

Billing will take place as per Billing Schedule.

If the above meets with your approval, please sign this letter and return one copy to us.

Cordially,

ACCEPTED AND
APPROVED_____
Date_____

The Worksheet

When planning and ordering items or services, you will want to prepare a separate worksheet for each purchase or work order. List all the details of a purchase or a work order along with the cost of each item and service. Refer to the SAMPLE OF A WORKSHEET for help

The information you gather on your worksheet will be transferred to the estimate/invoice you will give to your client and the purchase order you will give to your vendor or contractor. Any commission you are charging out to your client, as well as applicable sales tax on purchases and services, will be Included on your worksheet and estimate/invoice. The worksheet, therefore, is your way of keeping track of incoming and outgoing monies.

Client: Richardson

WORKSHEET

INSTYLE DECOR

Interior Design & Decorating

222 Durham St., Stratford, ON

ESTIMATE DESCRIPTION	NET UNIT	NET TOTAL
- 2 pieces 14', 1 piece 16', 1 piece 12' "Ogee" Crown Moulding (56 linear ft. @ $3.00 per linear ft.)	3.00	168.00
- 1 piece 16', 1 piece 12', 1 piece 10', 6" wide "French" baseboard (38 linear ft. @ $1.73 per linear ft.)	1.73	65.74

REMARKS: Please notify when ready for delivery

P.O. No.	Supplier	Item	List Unit	List Total	Comm 25%	Selling Price	Tax .08%	Selling Price
127	Duro Build	Crown Moulding	3.00	168.00	33.60	201.60	16.13	217.73
127	Duro Build	Baseboard	1.73	65.74	16.44	82.18	6.58	88.75

SAMPLE OF A WORKSHEET

© Copyright 2013

Interior Design For Today

Your Own Interior Design Business

You have developed your decorating skills, gotten an overview of the interior design work project, been instructed in building relationship with pre-clients and trades people, and studied various methods of charging out your services as an Interior Designer. All these aspects of interior design are beneficial to you whether your intention is to decorate your own home or take on a few decorating jobs through friends and neighbors. However, if you intend to start your own Interior Design business you will need to market your skills.

In this lesson you will learn how to prepare and present yourself as a professional Interior Designer and set up **Your Own Interior Design Business** as well as *promote* and *advertise* it.

Starting your own Business

Preparatory Work

Before you launch into the Interior Design profession, you will want to prepare yourself for the industry. You will want to familiarize yourself with the ins and outs of the Interior Design marketplace.

Visit Design Centers and showrooms of various vendors and study what they have to offer. Learn of their way of doing business. Visit retail furniture outlets and familiarize yourself with purchasing options.

One way to gain experience in the industry is to decorate your own home. You will gain hands-on experience working with vendors and trades people and your own home will become your showplace as a reference to what you can do.

Before setting up your own design business, you may choose to gradually enter the field by working as a salesperson in a furniture or fabric store, apprentice for a decorator, or work as an associate of a successful design firm. All these options are available to you with the expertise gained through your studies of Interior Design and can help lead you to venture out on your own in the industry.

Setting Up Your Business

You have decided to run your own interior design business. Your first step is to meet with a knowledgeable lawyer and accountant to seek advice on how to set up your business, deciding on a sole proprietorship, partnership, limited partnership, or corporation. Depending on your set up, you may also want to meet with an insurance broker.

Once you have decided on the type and form of business set up you intend, and have followed the advice given you in setting it up, you are ready to market your interior design skills.

A Business Name

Your business name will reflect your intentions depending on the services you offer. If you open your own decorating shop and sell home decor merchandise as well as offer a decorating service, you will want to choose a name that will reflect this intention. If you intend to run a design studio, solely offering design services, you will want to choose a business name that highlights this area of expertise.

Once you have decided on the scope of your design business and have chosen an appropriate business name, you are ready to promote your services.

Your Work Place

Your attitude regarding your work place will define success or failure. Keep a positive outlook and prepare a work space that reflects this attitude. If you have chosen to set up an office in your home, set it up to reflect a good work ethic. Treat it as an office with a business atmosphere.

Provide for yourself a sufficient work surface, professional tools, and a functioning filing system to effectively keep records. Instead of a small drafting board, invest in a drafting table. Or, if you are apt, and can afford it, invest in a computer, printer, and a software program geared toward the interior design industry to help you draft up kitchen and bathroom designs, floorplans, and furniture layouts, as well as put together color palettes for rooms you are working on.

Outfit your office with a bookcase for reference books and a place to store your portfolio. Display interiors in framed artwork. Provide an attractive seating arrangement for clients and keep the space looking fresh and neat.

Locating Vendors & Trades People

In order to locate vendors and trades people in your area, you will have to do some footwork. Use the *Yellow Pages* of your telephone directory to scout

out those in the trades, study business ads in the local newspaper, contact local trade schools and community colleges, and talk to local vendors, asking for recommendations.

If purchasing furnishings from a furniture showroom, ask the manager for his recommendations for upholsterers, drapers, and carpenters.

To locate home fashion vendors, subscribe to decorating and home improvement magazines and study adds in the "Buyer's Guide" section.

Once you have located those who have to offer what you will be looking for, call each one, and make an appointment to meet and share your intentions to build a working relationship.

Promoting your Business

Business Stationery

Just as your business name reflects the area of expertise of your business, so will your business card and letterhead, but in more detail, and in a format that can be effectively used to promote your services.

Design your own logo or have a graphic designer design it for you. Include it in your business card as well as your name, address, telephone number, and in point form, highlight ed aspects of design you are promoting. Refer to the BUSINESS CARD SAMPLE at the end of this unit. A well-designed business card reflects your business attitude, so put time and effort into its preparation and go for a clear professional presentation.

Along with business cards, letterhead will also represent your expertise to the public. Incorporate your logo, name, business name, address and phone number in a neat, precise manner at the top of each 8½" x 11" page. This stationery will be used for correspondence with your clients, vendors, and trades people, to be sent out in a logo-ed envelope.

Another way to express and promote your business is through a pamphlet. The pamphlet is set up in a format that allows more detail of your expertise and intentions as an interior design firm. You might also want to include a simple schedule of design fees. Design it yourself, or have a graphic designer involved. This visual presentation will promote you as a well-organized business which will go a long way to impress your expertise upon the minds of pre-clients.

Each of these forms, once designed and a template made, can be printed up at a local print shop where choices in paper quality will be given to you. To get a professional "look," consider a professional quality paper.

Design Portfolio

Put together a portfolio of tear-sheets supplied by vendors and pamphlets displaying merchandise available. Gather magazine pictures of good design and have them available to show pre-clients.

Include in your portfolio a visual presentation of work you have done. Display your expertise in a series of pictures of interior designs you have been involved in creating, as well as publicity you have received for your work through write-ups or letters of recommendation.

Your involvement and previous job experience working as an assistant or apprentice for a decorator or design service can be reflected and displayed in your portfolio, as well as pictures of work you have done in your newly decorated home.

Keep design presentations of projects you have completed in your School of Design studies. These form the basis of presentation skills of design you have developed and will use on future jobs. Include these in your portfolio as well as your diploma at graduation.

Keep adding to your portfolio as you acquire and complete interior design projects for clients. Your portfolio is a powerful marketing tool that will be pivotal to your success as an interior designer and in the establishment of your interior design business.

Word-of-Mouth

In order to gain work in the interior design industry, you will have to aggressively promote your services. Having re-designed and decorated your own home, your own home becomes a "showroom." As you invite family and friends to your home, you are promoting your expertise.

If you have successfully applied your skills and knowledge in your home, those who come in will admire the work you have done and ask for help in redecorating their home, or the home of a friend once their knowledge of your expertise has been gained. You might consider helping a family member or friend without cost, recognizing that this is a viable form of promoting your business, that by word-of-mouth you will become known for your expertise and recommended to others. A good way to promote your new career as an interior designer, is to have a "home party." Invite neighbors and guests in for an evening of food and fellowship in your newly decorated home.

Share that you have graduated from an Interior Design school and have begun your own design business and leave it at that. Let your guests enjoy the beauty of your home, and as you mingle, offer decorating advice to those who share their decorating dilemmas. Each guest is a potential client or a lead to a client through word-of-mouth.

Public Relations

Another form of advertising your wares, is via public relations, building relationships with others with whom you can work along side. One source of contact is with the real estate industry.

Developing relationships with real estate brokers gives you access to vital information regarding those who might be interested in your services. Offer your expertise in the form of "staging." Present your business card and explain how you can be of service to their sellers, how you can help them speed up the selling process by a short-term commitment to up-date, re-locate furnishings, and present the seller's home in an attractive package.

Your expertise as an interior designer more than qualifies you as a stager. Rules regarding furniture layout, color, and design apply in re-design and "staging" a room just as they do in designing and decorating a space. The main difference in approach is to work with already existing furnishings, re-arranging them for most impact. Another "lead" in acquiring work, is to develop relations with home builders. Contact the builder or building manager for opportunity to furnish a model home. In the event you are contracted for the job, you will rent furnishings rather than purchase them, making your job easier. Have your business card available at showings. Though visitors may not purchase a home, they may decide to contact you for your services as an interior designer.

Take the opportunity to offer your expertise free of charge to furniture store owners. Offer to set up an attractive window display in exchange for acknowledgement that the display was done by your design firm.

Lectures

An effective lead to contracting interior design work is to give lectures at garden clubs, country clubs, and women's clubs. If opportunity arises, inform the local newspaper of this up-coming event.

Give talks on highlighted aspects of interior design, such as storage, window treatments, decorating trends, choosing a color scheme, or any other topic of interest related to your field of expertise. Use visuals and other material to interact with your audience, such as the "ICE BREAKER," or another questionnaire. Give a well-prepared presentation and have brochures and business cards available. This is a sure opportunity to expose yourself as a professional interior designer and to promote your interior design business.

BUSINESS CARD SAMPLE

Advertising your Business

Advertising Methods

It is absolutely necessary to advertise your business in order to be successful. However, you can cut advertising costs by carefully choosing advertising methods.

Yellow Pages

By listing your business services in the yellow pages of your local phone directory, you are able to target those seeking interior design services.

Choosing an add size that fits your budget is essential. Though your add should be professional, it does not have to be large. It does not have to compete with larger interior design adds, however, you will want to discover your niche and highlight your specialties. For instance, if other adds neglect to offer "staging," or re-design or simple design services, make one of these your specialty, along with other services you offer. Try to determine your competitive edge. Always offer a follow-up brochure and a free consultation to those who reply to your add.

Newspaper Adds

When you begin your business, advertising in large newspapers will be out of reach for you, however, consider advertising in the classified adds of a smaller community weekly paper or free circulation for economical exposure.

Direct Mail

Mail out flyers to potential clients, however, be selective in whom they are sent to. Target a certain "higher income" area in your community or other communities. Contact a list broker for lists of those who have recently purchased a new home or of doctors, lawyers, and other high-income professionals. Follow your local newspaper write-ups on newcomers to your community and inform them of your services.

To personalize your mail-out, set if up as a hand-signed letter of introduction to yourself and your design services, adding a brief handwritten personal note at the bottom. Include a simple brochure along with it, and mail it out in an addressed envelope. Use letterhead stationery for your letter, however enclose it in an unmarked envelope with your personal name in the return address. To have your letter distinguished from "junk mail," keep the envelope free of sales messages. Although this method is more expensive than a flyer, it has greater potential for response and warrants the extra expense.

A Web Presence

Designing and maintaining a web site advertising your business is another avenue of promotion. Make sure to keep it updated. Along with it provide a link for potential clients to subscribe to a monthly newsletter informing readers of ongoing projects and opportunities for them to solicit your expertise. So save on expense, check out free web spaces on-line. They provide everything you need to set up your web page. Tell about yourself and the services that you offer. Add colorful pictures of your work and encourage both standing and new clients that you are interested in keeping them informed.

Of course, having a web site that no one knows about will not prove productive so make sure to advertise your web site along with other modes of advertising.

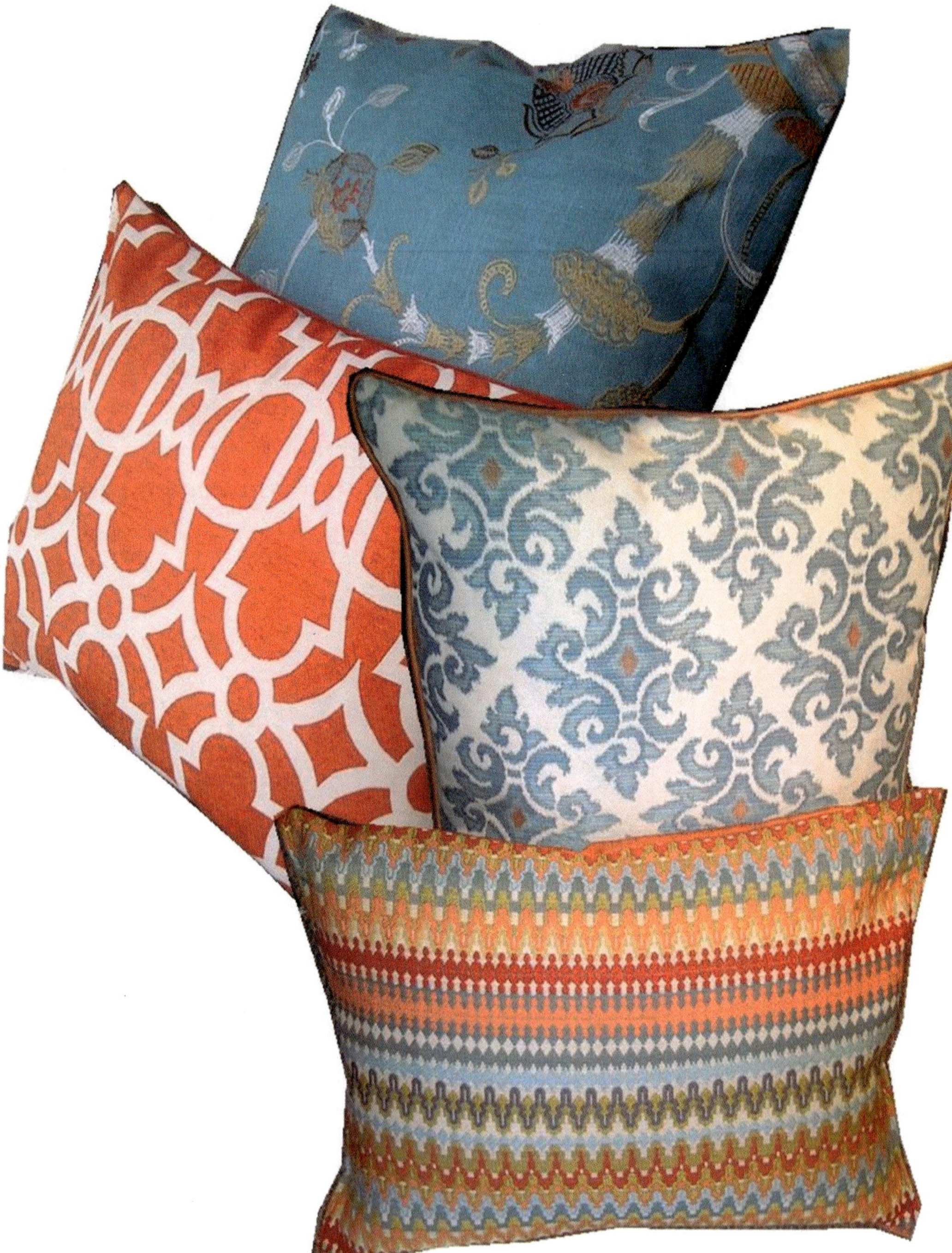

UNIT II DESIGN PROJECT Part C

1. Complete a **Kitchen Floorplan and Lighting Layout** of your own design for your kitchen or the kitchen of a friend.

    a. Complete a **KITCHEN DESIGN QUESTIONNAIRE** for your kitchen. Make a copy of the original and keep extra copies on file for future use.

    b. Draw a **Rough Sketch** of your kitchen space, referring to the following SAMPLE OF A ROUGH SKETCH. Indicate doors and the direction they swing, windows, heating/cooling units, electrical outlets, fixtures, and switches.

    c. Complete a **Kitchen Floorplan and Lighting Layout** of your kitchen. Center the to-scale drawing on ¼" Graph paper and photo copy onto letter stock. Consider positioning of the work triangle and guidelines for balance and best use of counter space. Add lighting to the floorplan. Refer to COUNTER SPACE & LIGHTING as well as the following SYMBOL CHART.

2. Complete a **Bathroom Floorplan and Lighting Layout** of your own design for your bathroom or the bathroom of a friend.

    a. Complete and submit a **BATHROOM DESIGN QUESTIONNAIRE** for your bathroom. Make a copy of the original and keep extra copies on file for future use.

    b. Draw a **Rough Sketch** of your bathroom space, referring to the SAMPLE OF A ROUGH SKETCH. Indicate doors and the direction they swing, windows, heating/cooling units, electrical outlets, fixtures, and switches.

    c. Complete a **Bathroom Floorplan and Lighting Layout** of your bathroom. Add lighting to the floorplan. Consider the basic layout, providing adequate space for each fixture. Refer to SAMPLE BATHROOM LAYOUTS A and SAMPLE BATHROOM LAYOUT B. Refer to the SYMBOL CHART for symbols.

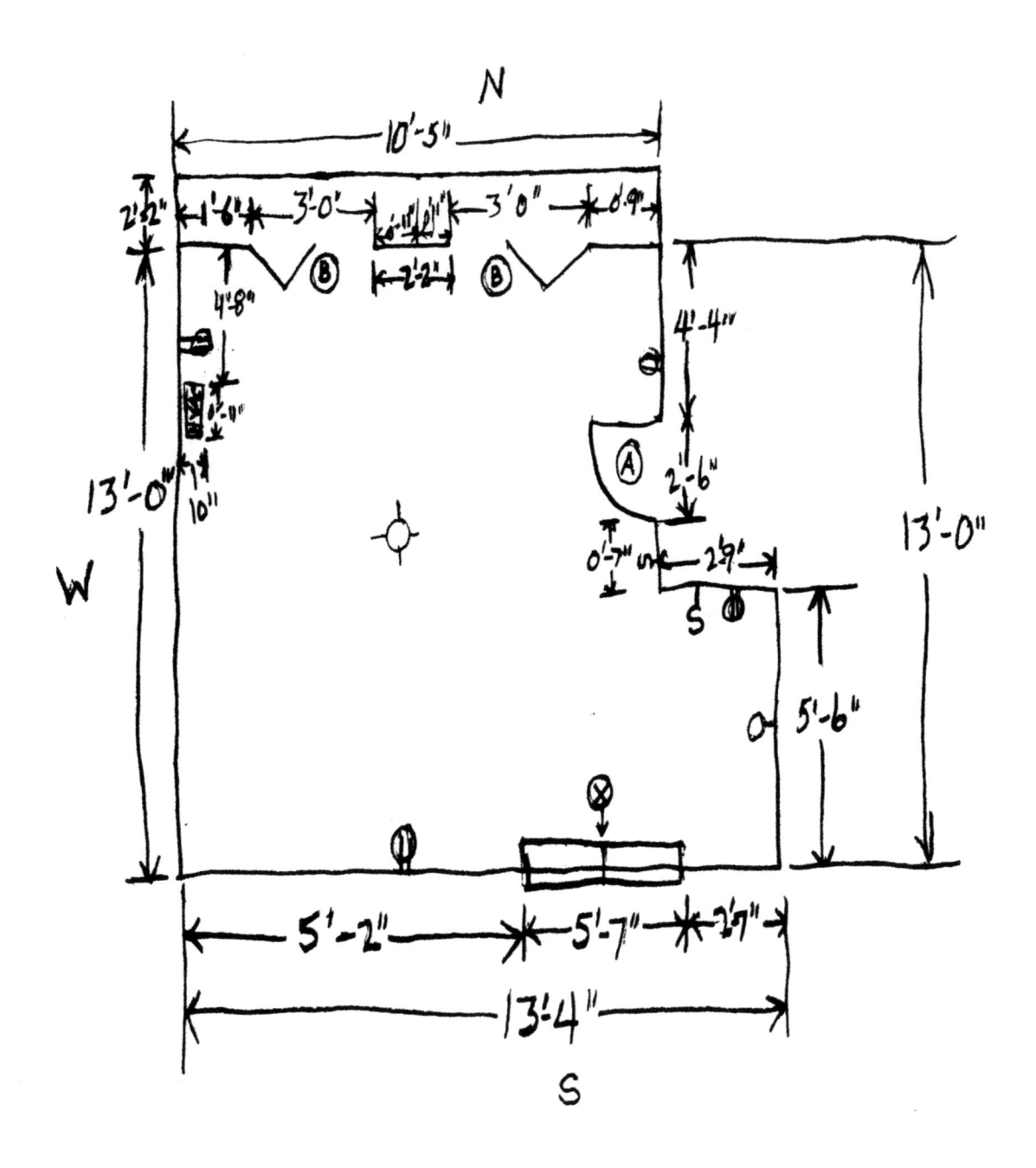

SAMPLE OF A ROUGH SKETCH

Wall Switch	Cable
S	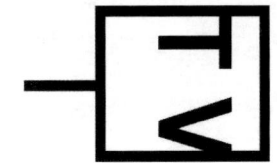 TV

Ceiling Outlet	Telephone Jack

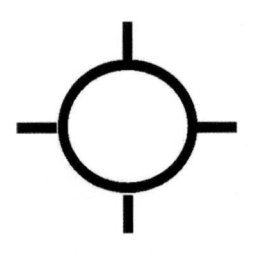

Base Outlet	Wall Outlet

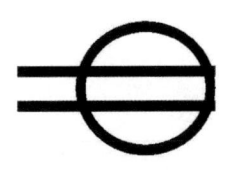

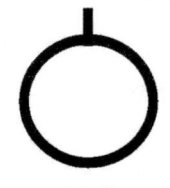

SYMBOL CHART

3. Complete a **FLOORPLAN PRESENTATION BOARD, COLOR SCHEME PRESENTATION BOARD, FURNITURE PRESENTATION BOARD**, and **WINDOW PRESENTATION BOARD** for each of your Living Room, Bedroom, and Dining Room, as well as for Stafford's Living/Dining Room. Complete a **BED TREATMENT BOARD** for your Bedroom.

   Reread your lesson entitled THE INTERIOR DESIGN PACKAGE PRESENTATION and refer to the DINING ROOM FLOORPLAN PRESENTATION BOARD, COLOR SCHEME PRESENTATION BOARD, FURNITURE PRESENTATION BOARD, WINDOW PRESENTATION BOARD, AND BED TREATMENT PRESENTATION BOARD.

   Use blank sheets of card stock. Label each board with the name of your client, the room you are working on, and the name of the display. If lettering by hand, keep lettering neat and all in one case for coherency. Use stick-on letters as an option.

   Use drawings and pictures, as well as paint and fabric samples, from your worksheets, or use new samples and make new drawings. Apply them to each board of card stock and mount them onto decorative backgrounds as shown in your helps.

4. Complete a **Budget Presentation** for each of your Living Room, Bedroom, and Dining Room, as well as for Stafford's Living/Dining Room projects. Refer to the BUDGET PRESENTATION sample. Format your presentation on 8½" x 11" letterhead. Include today's date, as well as your client's name and mailing address. Entitle it with the name of the room the budget is for and list each individual item and service along with its cost including detailed information.

   Visit your fabric supplier, local building center, and local vendors, for prices of merchandise to be purchased for your job. Contact drapers, upholsterers, carpenters, and other tradespeople for estimates. Keep quotes as accurate as possible.

5. Compile **Room Style, Furniture Style, Color Style** Charts. Cut out pictures from magazines and compile them into albums. Choose pictures of rooms in a variety of styles, as well as those displaying a variety of furniture styles and those in a variety of color combinations. Refer to suggestions in Brackets on the "ICE BREAKER." File these charts for you own use.

"ICE BREAKER"

Name: _____ Date: _____

Address: _____

Phone Number: _____

DECORATING STYLE

1. Describe your decorating style.
   _____

2. What would be your reason to use my services, Interior Design, Redesign, or Staging?
   _____

3. What is the main room of your concern? (Go there)
   _____

4. What do you like about this room? Why? (Determine style, color mood)
   _____

5. What don't you like about it? Why?
   _____

6. Are you happy with the floor covering? If not, would you consider changing it?
   _____

7. What pieces of furniture would you keep? Why? (Determine style, color preference)
   _____

8. What pieces would you be willing to part with? Why?
   _____
   _____

9. If the pieces could be affordably revamped, would you consider keeping them?
   _____

Interior Design For Today © Copyright 2013

FURNITURE PLACEMENT

1. What kinds of activity take place in this room? Does the furniture in this room meet all those needs? If not, what is still needed?

   _____

STYLE & COLOR

Room Style Charts
   Have Pre-Client choose 2 rooms they prefer.

1. What do you like about these rooms? (Determine style, ie. Victorian, Art Deco, Contemporary, Traditional, etc.)

   Room A_____

   _____

   Room B_____

   _____

2. How do these rooms make you feel? (Determine the style and color mood, ie. stoic, formal, sophisticated, warm, friendly.

   Room A_____

   _____

   Room B_____

FURNITURE STYLE

Furniture Style Chart
   Check off Pre-Client's choices. (Determine furniture style, ie. elaborate, antique, simple-lined, etc.)

   A____ B____ C____ D____ E____ F____ G____ H____

Color Combo Chart
   Check off Pre-Client's choices. (Determine Monochromatic, Muted Complementary, Vibrant Contrast)

   A____ B____ C____ D____ E____ F____ G____ H____

© Copyright 2013

Copyright© 2013, All rights reserved

Made in the USA
San Bernardino, CA
16 April 2014